THE ABUNDANT LIFE
BIBLE
AMPLIFIER

HOSEA–MICAH

JON L. DYBDAHL

THE ABUNDANT LIFE
BIBLE
AMPLIFIER

HOSEA–
MICAH

**A Call to
Radical Reform**

GEORGE R. KNIGHT
General Editor

Pacific Press Publishing Association
Boise, Idaho
Oshawa, Ontario, Canada

Edited by B. Russell Holt
Designed by Tim Larson
Typeset in 11/14 Janson Text

Unless otherwise mentioned, all Bible quotations in this book are from the New International Version, and all emphasis in Bible quotations is supplied by the author.

Library of Congress Cataloging-in-Publication Data:

Dybdahl, Jon.
    Hosea-Micah : a call to radical reform / Jon L. Dybdahl : [edited by] George R. Knight, B. Russell Holt.
        p.   cm. — (The abundant life Bible amplifier)
    Includes bibliographical references.
    ISBN 0-8163-1362-8 (cloth : alk. paper). — ISBN 0-8163-1358-X (pbk. : alk. paper)
    1. Bible. O.T. Minor Prophets—Criticism, interpretation, etc.
I. Knight, George R. II. Holt, B. Russell. III. Title. IV. Series.
BS1560.D93 1996
224'.907—dc20   96-28859
                                                            CIP

96 97 98 99 00 • 5 4 3 2 1

CONTENTS

General Preface 9
Author's Preface 11
How to Use This Book 13
Introduction to Hosea-Micah 17
List of Works Cited 25

Part I: Hosea: The Anguish of Steadfast Love
1. Introduction to Hosea 31
2. A Wayward Wife and a Hurting Husband (1–3) 36
3. A Wayward Israel (4–10) 51
4. A Loving Lord (11–14) 66

Part II: Joel: Facing the Day of the Lord
5. Introduction to Joel 83
6. Facing the Day of the Lord (1–3) 87

Part III: Amos: Judgment on Injustice, Perversion, and Pride
7. Introduction to Amos 105
8. Prophecies Against the Nations and Israel (1:1–5:17) 109
9. Exile, Divine Retribution, and Restoration (5:18–9:15) 124

Part IV: Obadiah: Arrogant Edom Falls
10. Introduction to Obadiah 143
11. Arrogant Edom Falls (1) 147

Part V: Jonah: God's Missionary Heart
12. Introduction to Jonah 157
13. The Human Missionary Flees (1, 2) 162
14. The Divine Missionary Persists (3, 4) 173

Part VI: Micah: Gloom, Yet Greater Glory
15. Introduction to Micah 189
16. False Leaders Fail (1–4) 194
17. A Righteous Ruler Reigns (5–7) 208

DEDICATION

To our children:

Jonna and Monty
Paul and Kristyn
Krista and Randy

With thanks and love inexpressible.

GENERAL PREFACE

The Abundant Life Bible Amplifier series is aimed at helping readers understand the Bible better. Rather than merely offering comments on or about the Bible, each volume seeks to enable people to study their Bibles with fuller understanding.

To accomplish that task, scholars who are also proven communicators have been selected to author each volume. The basic idea underlying this combination is that scholarship and the ability to communicate on a popular level are compatible skills.

While the Bible Amplifier is written with the needs and abilities of laypeople in mind, it will also prove helpful to pastors and teachers. Beyond individual readers, the series will be useful in church study groups and as guides to enrich participation in the weekly prayer meeting.

Rather than focusing on the details of each verse, the Bible Amplifier series seeks to give readers an understanding of the themes and patterns of each biblical book as a whole and how each passage fits into that context. As a result, the series does not seek to solve all the problems or answer all the questions that may be related to a given text. In the process of accomplishing the goal for the series, both inductive and explanatory methodologies are used.

Each volume in this series presents its author's understanding of the biblical book being studied. As such, it does not necessarily represent the "official" position of the Seventh-day Adventist Church.

It should be noted that the Bible Amplifier series utilizes the New International Version of the Bible as its basic text. *Every reader should read the "How to Use This Book" section to get the fullest benefit from the Bible Amplifier study volumes.*

Dr. Jon Dybdahl, chairperson of the Department of World Mission at the Seventh-day Adventist Theological Seminary at Andrews University, holds a doctoral degree in Old Testament from Fuller

Theological Seminary. Prior to his current assignment, Dr. Dybdahl servied as a pastor, a professor of Old Testament at Walla Walla College, a missionary in Southeast Asia, and the director of the Seventh-day Adventist Institute of World Mission. He has authored several other books, including, *Old Testament Grace* and *Exodus: God Creates a People* in The Abundant Life Bible Amplifier series.

George R. Knight
Berrien Springs, Michigan

AUTHOR'S PREFACE

At Walla Walla College in the mid-80s I began teaching a class on the Hebrew prophets, but never dreamt of writing a book on the subject. I merely tried to keep one day ahead of my students. They pushed me to do the work that got me started on a lifelong journey with these radical Israelite revivalists, a journey that won't end. This book is only a part of that journey, and it is a simple invitation to you to go on that trip as well. I'm convinced that the longer you listen to these preachers of renewal, the more you will appreciate them. Even if you don't always like what they say or how they say it, you can't help but be moved by their spirit and deep commitment.

Special thanks to general editor George Knight for his marvelous work on this Bible Amplifier series. His gentle and insistent encouragement and guidance have been invaluable to me.

The courage of Pacific Press to initiate this series and its ongoing dedication to it are commendable. This has been a source of strength to me. The desire to publish material that leads people to in-depth Bible study is Spirit inspired.

All authors know that their work is really a community endeavor. Spouses, children, co-workers, and employers all make some adjustments to enable the work to be done. My gratitude goes to my wonderful family, my colleagues at the Institute of World Mission, the Secretariat of the General Conference, and Andrews University. Special thanks to my students who kept asking questions about the prophets because they wanted to understand them. My prayer is that you, the reader, will continue that wonderful practice as you interact with the prophets—and with me—in the pages that follow.

Jon L. Dybdahl
Berrien Springs, Michigan

How to Use This Book

The Abundant Life Amplifier series treats each major portion of each Bible book in five main sections.

The first section is called "Getting Into the Word." The purpose of this section is to encourage readers to study their own Bibles. For that reason, the text of the Bible has not been printed in the volumes in this series.

You will get the most out of your study if you work through the exercises in each of the "Getting Into the Word" sections. This will not only aid you in learning more about the Bible but will also increase your skill in using Bible tools and in asking (and answering) meaningful questions about the Bible.

It will be helpful if you write out the answers and keep them in a notebook or file folder for each biblical book. Writing out your thoughts will enhance your understanding. The benefit derived from such study, of course, will be proportionate to the amount of effort expended.

The "Getting Into the Word" sections assume that the reader has certain minimal tools available. Among these are a concordance and a Bible with maps and marginal cross-references. If you don't have a New International Version of the Bible, we recommend that you obtain one for use with this series, since all the Bible Amplifier authors are using the NIV as their basic text. For the same reason, your best choice of a concordance is the *NIV Exhaustive Concordance*, edited by E. W. Goodrick and J. R. Kohlenberger. Strong's *Exhaustive Concordance of the Bible* and Young's *Analytical Concordance to the Bible* are also useful. However, even if all you have is Cruden's *Concordance*, you will be able to do all of the "Getting Into the Word" exercises and most of the "Researching the Word" exercises.

The "Getting Into the Word" sections also assume that the reader has a Bible dictionary. The *Seventh-day Adventist Bible Dictionary* is quite helpful, but those interested in greater depth may want to acquire the four-volume *International Standard Bible Encyclopedia* (1974-1988 edition) or the six-volume *Anchor Bible Dictionary*.

The second section in the treatment of the biblical passages is called "Exploring the Word." The purpose of this section is to discuss the major themes in each biblical book. Thus the comments will typically deal with fairly large portions of Scripture (often an entire chapter) rather than providing a verse-by-verse treatment, such as is found in the *Seventh-day Adventist Bible Commentary*. In fact, many verses and perhaps whole passages in some biblical books may be treated minimally or passed over altogether.

Another thing that should be noted is that the purpose of the "Exploring the Word" sections is not to respond to all the problems or answer all the questions that might arise in each passage. Rather, as stated above, the "Exploring the Word" sections are to develop the Bible writers' major themes. In the process, the author of each volume will bring the best of modern scholarship into the discussion and thus enrich the reader's understanding of the biblical passage at hand. The "Exploring the Word" sections will also develop and provide insight into many of the issues first raised in the "Getting Into the Word" exercises.

The third section in the treatment of the biblical passage is "Applying the Word." This section is aimed at bringing the lessons of each passage into daily life. Once again, you may want to write out a response to these questions and keep them in your notebook or file folder on the biblical book being studied.

The fourth section, "Researching the Word," is for those students who want to delve more deeply into the Bible passage under study or into the history behind it. It is recognized that not everyone will have the research tools for this section. Those expecting to use the research sections should have an exhaustive Bible concordance, the *Seventh-day Adventist Bible Commentary*, a good Bible dictionary, and a Bible atlas. It will also be helpful to have several versions of the Bible.

The final component in each chapter of this book will be a list of recommendations for "Further Study of the Word." While most readers will not have all of these works, many of them may be available in local libraries. Others can be purchased through your local book dealer. It is assumed that many users of this series will already own the seven-volume *Seventh-day Adventist Bible Commentary* and the one-volume *Seventh-day Adventist Bible Dictionary*.

In closing, it should be noted that while a reader will learn much about the Bible from a *reading* of the books in the Bible Amplifier series, he or she will gain infinitely more by *studying* the Bible in connection with that reading.

Introduction to Hosea–Micah

Prophets are radicals. Their radical nature shows itself in the strong flavor of their language, as well as in the often extreme actions and lifestyles they manifest. This radical style fits their mission and the times in which they live. Critical historical situations and calls for reform demand leaders who are not afraid to be different from the crowd.

Don't let strong words and disturbing ideas turn you away from the prophets. Persist in patiently listening to these words from an earlier era, and you will find them becoming amazingly relevant to your present world. The contemporary Word of God to Israel and Judah remains a living Word today. We can still learn much from the six prophets this book deals with. If we allow them to speak to us, these radical reformers can have an important part in renewing God's church today.

The Book of the Twelve

For the Jews, the six small prophetic books covered by this volume (Hosea, Joel, Amos, Obadiah, Jonah, and Micah) made up the first half of a single scroll. Jews called this scroll the "Book of the Twelve" because of the twelve prophetic books contained in it. The last half of the scroll consisted of the other six small books that complete the Old Testament—Nahum through Malachi. This scroll containing the writings of the Twelve was about the same size as each of the prophetic scrolls of Jeremiah, Isaiah, or Ezekiel.

Exactly when these twelve individual books were gathered into one scroll we do not know. The apocryphal book, Ecclesiasticus (dating from about 200 B.C.), already mentions the Twelve as a unit, so by that time, at least, the process was well underway. This means that about two centuries after Malachi, the last prophet of the Twelve, these books had already been brought together.

Unfortunately, many people call these prophets "minor prophets." This implies that they are less crucial than the major prophets such as Isaiah, Jeremiah, or Ezekiel. The term *minor*, however originally referred to the small size of these books in contrast to the length of the books written by the major prophets. Certainly the inspiration and importance of these smaller prophetic books is in no way less than that of their more lengthy Old Testament counterparts.

We are not sure exactly why the twelve books were arranged in their present order, although many suggest it has to do, at least in part, with chronology. With one possible exception, the Hosea-Micah block of books that we are studying in this volume dated from an earlier period than the last six books of the Twelve.

Evidence seems to suggest that the six books we are studying circulated independently as a collection prior to being grouped at a later time with the rest of the Twelve (Stuart, xliv). Part of the evidence for this is that the Greek Old Testament (the Septuagint, or LXX) has these six books in a slightly different order than they appear in the Hebrew Old Testament. The last six books of the Twelve appear in the same order in both Greek and Hebrew versions.

The six books—Hosea through Micah—date from the early period of the prophets, which was the time of Assyrian domination. This Mesopotamian power, centered just north of Babylon, was prominent during the Neo-Assyrian period, which is usually dated from 900 to 612 B.C. At a later point in this chapter, we will discuss more details of this period of history.

Although scholars are not agreed on the exact dates, these six books can be dated approximately as follows (see Nichol, 4:18): Hosea, 755–725 B.C.; Joel, 620 B.C.; Amos, 767–753 B.C.; Obadiah, 585 B.C. (or possibly ninth century B.C.; see Nichol, 4:22); Jonah, 790

B.C.; Micah, 740–700 B.C. This means that all these books, with the exception of Obadiah, were written during the Neo-Assyrian period. In general, the last six books of the Twelve came from a later period.

Some important early Greek manuscripts place the Book of the Twelve before the major prophets Isaiah, Jeremiah, and Ezekiel. The Hebrew Bible, however, places the Twelve at the end of the Old Testament prophetic writings, where they form a fitting conclusion. Major modern versions do the same.

This means that, in the thinking of the Jews, the six prophets we are studying form the first half of the last prophetic "book" of the Bible. Seeing these writers in this light helps us visualize them as uniting in an overall message as they form the opening section of God's last Old Testament prophetic appeal to Israel.

The Historical Situation

The specific historical background for each book will be given in the Introduction to that book, however, some general comments can profitably be made here. In broad strokes, what is happening during the period when these books were being written?

All the prophets we are considering wrote after the division of the Israelite nation into two separate kingdoms. Beginning 931 B.C. after the death of Solomon, the Jews existed as two nations—the northern kingdom of Israel and the southern kingdom of Judah. David's descendants ruled the southern kingdom, while the northern kingdom of Israel set up its own royal line. The southern capital was in Jerusalem, while the kings of the northern territory ruled mostly from Samaria.

Three of our books—Hosea, Amos, and Jonah—were written to the northern kingdom; the other three—Obadiah, Joel, and Micah—were written to the southern kingdom. The introductory verses of Hosea, Amos, and Micah mention the names of Hebrew kings who reigned during the time these prophets wrote. The interested reader can go to the books of Chronicles and Kings or to other sources and find out specific details of the reign of each king.

Even a cursory reading of Hosea through Micah will make it clear that this period was a difficult one for the Jews. Social, political, and, in particular, religious problems plagued her. The prophets did not shrink from addressing all the problems the nation faced.

Both Israel and Judah faced enormous pressure from outside. Palestine's strategic geographic location between Egypt on the south and Mesopotamia to the north made life difficult for Israelites. Eventually both Jewish nations succumbed to conquest and were forced to disperse. Assyria conquered the northern kingdom of Israel in 722 B.C. and deported most of its people. Judah lasted approximately 125 years longer but eventually was conquered by Babylon between 605 and 586 B.C.

The dominant foreign power lying in the background of our six books is Assyria. Although Assyria had been around since the second millennium B.C., she really came into her golden age during the Neo-Assyrian period (900–612 B.C.). During this era she enlarged her territory from her northern Mesopotamian heartland to include Babylon, Media, Syro-Palestine, and even the Nile valley as far south as Thebes (Achtemeier, 108, 109).

Assyria touches the Old Testament story in many places. At no less than thirteen historical points between the years 853–627 B.C., Old Testament kings or events connect directly with Assyrian events, kings, and dates (Crim, 75). Both northern and southern kingdoms as well as various kings of the Israelites were part of the contact.

Although the Assyrians were polytheistic, the king was viewed as the regent (agent and representative) of the national god Ashur. The ruler regularly reported his activities, most often war, to this god. "Thus the Assyrian campaigns were conceived, at least in part, as a holy war against those who failed to avow his sovereignty" (Douglas, 104). As a national and religious duty, those who rebelled were ruthlessly pursued and punished.

Conquered territories were expected to be not only vassals or slave/subjects of Assyria, but vassal-subjects of Ashur, the national god, as well. Assyrian control was thus not only military-political, but also religious. Offenders and rebels were severely punished. During this Neo-Assyrian period, Assyria often followed the practice of deporting subject peoples, moving social groups around like so many pieces on a chessboard. In part, this was an attempt to lessen the opportunity to rebel. Such deportation befell the northern kingdom of Israel when she was conquered by Assyria in 722 B.C.

This fearsome Assyrian political/religious power lies behind so much of what is said in Hosea through Micah that we must keep it ever in mind. It pervaded the thinking of these prophets in much the same way that the cold war and Communism lay behind so much of European and North American words and actions from the late 1940s to the early 1990s.

Prophets and Prophecy

Since Hosea through Micah are prophetic writings, we can profit from understanding something of the nature of prophets and prophecy. We also need to examine the role they played in the life of the community of Israel.

The prophetic ministry is a crucial one in Scripture. Various forms of the word *prophet* occur more than 660 times in the Bible, with two-thirds of them being in the Old Testament (Jensen, *Israel*, 8). The prophetic writings, which consist of the former prophets (Joshua, Judges, 1 and 2 Samuel, 1 and 2 Kings) and the latter prophets (Isaiah, Jeremiah, Ezekiel, and the Book of the Twelve), are larger by far than either of the other two major sections of the Old Testament, the Torah (Pentateuch) and the Writings (the remainder of the Old Testament).

Debate has raged over the meaning of the word *prophet* but most scholars now see the Hebrew verb root (*nb'*) as meaning "to call." The basic meaning of the word *prophet*, then, would be "one called" or in particular "one called by God" (La Sor, Hubbard, and Bush, 299). The prophet who is called by God becomes God's mouthpiece and speaks for Him. The clearest exposition of this concept is in Exodus (see 4:14-16 and 17:1, 2) where Moses is likened to God, and Aaron, his spokesman, is called his prophet.

Some students of Scripture have viewed prophets mainly as "foretellers"—predictors of the future that God has in store. Other scholars have maintained that the prophets were primarily "forthtellers"—preachers who frankly declared God's message to His people in their present situation. Most believe that, in fact, the prophetic work included both of these functions, for the two complement each other. As one reads the prophets, however, it seems clear that specific future predictions do not form as large a part of their writings as some might think.

However, the prophets do make many predictions. Some deal with the fulfillment of events in the near future. These often are related to judgments on sin. Other predictions have to do with events further in the future dealing with the end time and/or the coming of the kingdom of God. These latter predictions often concern the restoration of God's people and are full of hope.

The question of how to interpret the predictions dealing with Israel's future is a challenging one. This is especially true with the prophecies that foretell restoration. In fact, most Bible students agree that the majority of specific restoration prophecies made to Israel by the prophets were *never* fulfilled (Nichol, 4:25-38). Various explanations have been advanced.

This book accepts the following explanation. Most of the promises and predictions the prophets made to Israel originally applied to the actual nation of Israel existing in the prophet's time. If Israel had been obedient and loyal to God, these predictions would have been fulfilled as given (see Deut. 28-30). Israel's disobedience kept God from doing what He desired (see Jer. 18:5-10). Therefore, what God wanted to do for and through ancient Israel will now be accomplished in general outline through the church, the new spiritual Israel (see Gal. 3:14, 28, 29; Rom. 9:30, 31). Paul develops this argument in Romans 9–11. In principle the prophecies that were originally for Israel will be fulfilled through the church during the present time and at the end of time. Although literal Assyria and Babylon may no longer threaten God's people, spiritual Babylon still does so, and God will deal with this threat too. Jesus Christ is the great "Yes" to all God's promises and dreams expressed by His spokesmen, the prophets (see Gal. 3:22). This concept will be developed further in the pages of this volume.

One more important issue must be considered before we leave the subject of prophets and prophecy. What is the main role prophets played in the life of God's people? What did they do?

For much of the last 100 years, people believed that the prophets were creatively original in their writings. The idea was that the prophets invented Old Testament ethics and gave birth to many of the covenant ideas found in the Pentateuch.

Evidence and recent scholarship clearly point away from this idea. The prophets deliberately go directly back to the covenant writings in the Pentateuch. The task of the prophets is to reform and renew—not to create. Their task, as they see it, is to call people back to obedience and faithfulness to the covenant given long before. Their call to reform is not radical in the sense of being new, rather it is radical because the people have strayed so far from God.

In particular, the prophets want to remind Israel of the blessings and cursings contained in the covenant (see Deut. 28–30). The judgments these prophets pronounce are based on and related to the covenant curses. The restoration they prophesy is founded on the covenant blessings Yahweh has given long ago. They speak mainly of how God's people may expect to be treated, based on the covenant God gave through Moses long before.

The prophets' basic analysis is that Israel has strayed far from Yahweh and the covenant. So many curses apply that judgment is a major topic. The real call, however, is for reform. Reformation can lead to covenant blessings and hope. That is, of course, the basis for my subtitle of this book, *A Call to Radical Reform*. Join us as we together seek to discover both what the prophets meant then and what they mean today.

■ Further Study of the Word

1. **For an introduction to the subject of prophets and prophecy, see W. S. Lasor, et al., eds., *Old Testament Survey*, 298-306.**
2. **Those who are interested in a more in-depth analysis of how to understand prophecies dealing with the future of**

Israel should read F. D. Nichol, ed. *Seventh-day Adventist Bible Commentary*, 4:25-38.

3. For a reference listing and classifying the types of curses and blessings contained in the Pentateuch, see Douglas Stuart, *Hosea-Jonah*, xxxii-xliii.

LIST OF WORKS CITED

Achtemeier, Paul J., ed. *Harper's Bible Dictionary*. San Francisco: Harper & Row, 1985.

Alexander, Desmond, David W. Baker, and Bruce Waltke. *Obadiah, Jonah, Micah: An Introduction and Commentary*. Tyndale Old Testament Commentaries. Downer's Grove, Ill.: InterVarsity Press, 1988.

Allen, Leslie C. *The Books of Joel, Obadiah, Jonah, and Micah*. The New International Commentary on the Old Testament. Grand Rapids, Mich.: William B. Eerdmans Publishing Company, 1976.

———. *Hosea-Malachi*. Washington, Penn.: Christian Literature Crusade, 1987.

Anderson, Bernhard W. *The Eighth Century Prophets*. Philadelphia: Fortress Press, 1978.

Barker, Kenneth, et al., eds. *The NIV Study Bible*. Grand Rapids, Mich.: Zondervan, 1985.

Beeley, Ray. *Amos*. London: The Banner of Truth Trust, 1969.

Brodsky, Harold. "An Enormous Horde Arranged for Battle: Locusts in the Book of Joel." *Bible Review* (August 1990): 32-39.

Corbett, J. Elliot. *The Prophets on Main Street*. Atlanta, Ga.: John Knox, 1977.

Crim, Keith, ed. *The Interpreter's Dictionary of the Bible*. Supplementary vol. Nashville, Tenn.: Abingdon Press, 1976.

Davies, G. I. *Hosea*. The New Century Bible Commentary. Grand Rapids, Mich.: Eerdmans/Marshall Pickering, 1992.

De Vaux, Roland. *Ancient Israel*. 2 vols. New York: McGraw Hill, 1965.

Douglas, J. D., ed. *The New Bible Dictionary*. Grand Rapids, Mich.: William B. Eerdmans Publishing Company, 1962.

Dybdahl, Jon L. *Israelite Village Land Tenure: Settlement to Exile*. Ann Arbor, Mich.: University Microfilms International, 1982.

———. *Old Testament Grace.* Boise, Idaho: Pacific Press Publishing Assn., 1990.

Fiddes, Paul S. "The Cross of Hosea Revisited: The Meaning of Suffering in the Book of Hosea." *Review and Expositor*, 90 (1993): 175-189.

Hasel, Gerhard F. *Jonah: Messenger of the Eleventh Hour.* Boise, Idaho: Pacific Press Publishing Assn., 1976.

———. *Understanding the Book of Amos: Basic Issues in Current Interpretations.* Grand Rapids, Mich.: Baker, 1991.

Horn, Siegfried H., ed. *Seventh-day Adventist Bible Dictionary.* Hagerstown, Md.: Review and Herald Publishing Assn., 1960.

Hubbard, David Allan. *Hosea: An Introduction and Commentary.* Tyndale Old Testament Commentaries. Downers Grove, Ill.: InterVarsity Press, 1989.

———. *Themes From the Minor Prophets.* Ventura, Calif.: Regal Books, 1977.

Jensen, Irving L. *Minor Prophets of Israel.* A Self-Study Guide. Chicago: Moody, 1975.

———. *Minor Prophets of Judah.* A Self-Study Guide. Chicago: Moody, 1975.

Kidner, Derek. *The Message of Hosea: Love to the Loveless.* Downers Grove, Ill.: InterVarsity Press, 1981.

King, Philip J. *Amos, Hosea, Micah—An Archaeological Commentary.* Philadelphia: The Westminster Press, 1988.

Kunz, Marilyn and Catherine Schell. *Amos: Prophet of Life-Style.* Wheaton, Ill.: Tyndale House, 1978.

La Sor, William Sanford, David Allan Hubbard, and Frederic William Bush. *Old Testament Survey.* Grand Rapids, Mich.: William B. Eerdmans Publishing Company, 1982.

Limburg, James. *Hosea-Micah.* Interpretation: A Bible Commentary for Teaching and Preaching. Atlanta: John Knox Press, 1988.

McComiskey, Thomas Edward, ed. *The Minor Prophets: An Exegetical and Expository Commentary.* 2 vols. Grand Rapids, Mich.: Baker Books, 1992.

Morgan, Campbell G. *Hosea: The Heart and Holiness of God.* Westwood. N.J.: Fleming H. Revell Company, 1964.

Motyer, J. A. *Studying the Book of Amos*. Nashville, Tenn.: Broadman Press, 1966.

————. *The Day of the Lion: The Message of Amos*. London: InterVarsity Press, 1974.

Nichol, Francis D., ed. *The Seventh-day Adventist Bible Commentary*. Hagerstown, Md.: Review and Herald Publishing Assn., 1955.

Rice, Richard. *The Reign of God: An Introduction to Christian Theology From a Seventh-day Adventist Perspective*. Berrien Springs, Mich.: Andrews University Press, 1985.

Stuart, Douglas, *Hosea-Jonah*. Word Biblical Commentary. Waco, Tex.: Word Books, 1987.

Thompson, J. A. *Handbook of Life in Bible Times*. Leicester, England: InterVarsity Press, 1986.

Watts, John D. W. *The Books of Joel, Obadiah, Jonah, Nahum, Habakkuk, and Zephaniah*. The Cambridge Bible Commentary on the New English Bible. London: Cambridge University Press, 1975.

White, Ellen G. *Patriarchs and Prophets*. Boise, Idaho: Pacific Press Publishing Assn., 1958.

————. *Prophets and Kings*. Boise, Idaho: Pacific Press Publishing Assn., 1943.

Wiseman, D. J. "Jonah's Nineveh." *Tyndale Bulletin*, 30 (1979): 29-51.

PART ONE

Hosea

The Anguish of
Steadfast Love

CHAPTER ONE

Introduction
to Hosea

Listening to Hosea tugs at the heartstrings. Anyone who has felt the pain of marital unfaithfulness or worried about his or her family will especially be touched. Hosea compares religious unfaithfulness to marital unfaithfulness. Hosea's own family experience parallels God's experience with His "wife," Israel.

When you care about a person or a relationship, you must respond to any threat to that relationship. You have to take action. In Hosea's book, both the prophet and God respond to unfaithfulness. Gomer and Israel have "played the prostitute." In such a situation, action is necessary but never easy. What Hosea and God do can be called "the anguished actions of steadfast love." This long-suffering love of both prophet and God lie behind all the words of this book.

■ Getting Into the Word

To get an overall feel for the book of Hosea, read it through, preferably at one sitting. As you read, look for answers to the following questions:

1. Can even judgment and punishment express love? How? Why? List the ways, both in word and deed, that Hosea and God express love.
2. What is God asking Hosea to do in this book? What is God asking Israel to do? What will be the result of these responses?

Hosea the Man

Hosea's name means "salvation" or "has saved." The name probably implies that God is the bringer of this salvation. Thus the name *Hosea* may be a shortened form of Joshua, meaning "Yahweh has saved" (see Num. 13:8). The Greek form of that name is, of course, Jesus. Thus Joshua, Hosea, and Jesus are simply three forms of the same name. The name of the last king of Israel (the northern kingdom) was also Hosea. Names can be confusing in the Old Testament!

Hosea's father's name is Beeri (1:1). The Hebrew terms, *son* and *father*, are both used rather loosely so that Beeri could be Hosea's father, grandfather, or even an important male ancestor. No other Scripture passage mentions the name Beeri, so we know very little about Hosea's family.

Neither do we know Hosea's hometown. The book uses many illustrations from agricultural and rural settings, causing some to speculate that Hosea was raised in a country environment. Whether he was born in the countryside or not, he is clearly familiar with it.

We are not even sure which of the two kingdoms—Judah or Israel—Hosea lived in during his ministry. His prominent mention of certain kings of Judah does not make it certain that Hosea belonged to the southern kingdom; he could have been a native northerner from Israel who later moved or fled to the southern kingdom of Judah. Some believe he did so after Samaria, Israel's capital, fell in 722 B.C.

Historical Setting

Hosea's ministry spanned about twenty-five years from 750-725 B.C., although the dates are somewhat open to question. The book of Hosea mentions the four kings of Judah that reigned during Hosea's ministry—Uzziah, Jotham, Ahaz, and Hezekiah (1:1)—but mentions only one king of Israel—Jereboam (II). In fact, six other kings also reigned in the northern kingdom during this period—

Zechariah, Shallum, Pekahiah, Pekah, Menahem, and Hosea! Due
to the political unrest and intrigue of the period, four of these six
were assassinated while in office by their successors and one (Hosea)
was captured. Only Menahem was succeeded in the regular way by
his son. Perhaps this shameful anarchy is the reason for leaving their
names out of the book. Or, if the prophet fled to Judah during this
period, then possibly he mentions the Judahite kings because they
played a more crucial role in his ministry.

Although Israel prospered economically under Jeroboam II, the
nation was in desperate straits politically. Assyria was a constant
threat, and various Israelite kings paid heavy tribute to her. Egypt
was also part of the political picture and had her supporters in Israel.
The competition between these two major powers certainly hurt
Israel. Their constant tug of war and Israel's struggle to perserve her
integrity drained the nation and finally ended in failure anyway. In
722 B.C. Israel fell to the Assyrians. Hosea was probably alive when
the fall came, but his book does not speak of it directly. His prophecies of destruction had already been written, and the fact that they
took place only confirmed the fulfillment of the divine prophetic
word through Hosea.

Even more important to Hosea than the political problems that
Israel faced was the religious condition of the people. Spiritually
and morally, the nation was bankrupt. Hosea repeatedly mentions
the idolatrous calf worship set up in the northern kingdom by
Jeroboam I (1 Kings 12). Apparently this idolatry continued, as well
as the more crude and inhumane worship later offered to the
Canaanite gods, Baal and Ashtoreth. Their worship involved child
sacrifice and gross sensuality (Nichol, 4:886). Hosea was appalled
by all this and reacted mightily against it.

During this time no commandment of God seemed to be kept.
Injustice and oppression were common. All levels of society, including rulers and priests, were involved. The situation was pervasive
and desperate.

Against this terrible background, Hosea made his appeal. His
strong words and obvious anguish become real and understandable
when we realize the situation he faced. Hosea's message was the *last*

divine appeal to the northern kingdom of Israel. When the message was unheeded, the resulting defeat of 722 B.C. was clearly seen as God's judgment on His people.

Theme and Message

The theme of Hosea is "The Anguish of Steadfast Love." The book is about Hosea's love life and God's steadfast love. If a person's love is temporary and fickle, then unreturned love, or rejection, presents no major problem. Fickle love can simply seek another object. However, when love is steadfast, rejection and unfaithfulness cause great anguish. Since love goes on while its object no longer returns any love, tremendous suffering results. Israel's unfaithfulness causes unspeakable anguish to God's heart of steadfast love. Hosea's own experience of having an unfaithful wife teaches him the pain in God's heart over Israel.

Hosea presents this message using two different communication techniques. Technique one is to use Hosea's own family life as a parable or illustration of the Israel-God relationship (chapters 1–3). Hosea's wife, Gomer, is unfaithful. Israel is unfaithful to God. This puts Hosea in God's position. God asks Hosea to manifest steadfast love in his family situation so that he—and we—can perhaps begin to understand how God must feel when Israel sins.

Technique two is to preach passionate sermons describing how God feels about Israel's unfaithfulness and what it will lead to (chapters 4–14). The two major sermons, although scathing, end on notes of hope (see chapters 4–11 for sermon one and chapters 12–14 for sermon two). God's steadfast love does *not* want to let Israel go. In spite of Israel's sin, God's love continues. Restoration is possible to those who return to Yahweh.

The following is an outline of the content of the entire book:

Outline of Hosea
The Anguish of Steadfast Love

I. A Wayward Wife and a Hurting Husband (Hosea 1–3)
   A. Superscription (1:1)
   B. Hosea's family (1:2-11)
   C. Comparison with Israel (2:1-23)
   D. Hosea reconciles with Gomer (3:1-5)
II. A Wayward Israel and a Loving Lord (Hosea 4–14)
   A. A wayward Israel (4:1–10:15)
      1. Israel's unfaithfulness (4:1–6:3)
      2. Israel's punishment (6:4–10:15)
   B. A loving Lord (11:1–14:9)
      1. God's love for Israel (11:1-11)
      2. Israel's punishment (11:12–13:16)
      3. Israel's restoration (14:1-9)

CHAPTER TWO

A Wayward Wife and a Hurting Husband

Hosea 1–3

The Old Testament world often seems strange to us. Chronologically and culturally distant, its images and stories often need special interpretation to become relevant. Hosea is an exception. This tale of an immoral spouse who leaves her husband and children to be with her lover immediately strikes us as relevant. Unfaithful husbands and wives, broken marriages, and abandoned children are all too familiar to us. We can easily identify with the heartbreak and deep emotions portrayed in the story.

The initial three chapters of Hosea form the basis for an extended development in the rest of the book. Chapters 1–3 spell out the story of Hosea's life with Gomer and their children. The first chapter explains the marriage and the children who join the family. Chapter 2 is a poem comparing Israel's unfaithfulness to God to that of an adulterous wife to her husband. The prophet clearly has in mind the idea that Israel's covenant with God is like a marriage. As Gomer is adulterous, so is Israel as she breaks her covenant with Yahweh. The second chapter concludes with God's reconciliation to erring Israel.

In chapter 3 Hosea is told to go and love Gomer and bring her back. The implication is that if God can be reconciled to an adulterous Israel, Hosea must do what is needed to be reunited in love with an immoral wife. Hosea must copy God. Hosea obeys the command and buys back an enslaved Gomer.

For Hosea, the prophetic call was costly. He was not simply to speak the words of Yahweh; he was chosen to live out the message and embody it in his actual life. Try to sense at a deep level what this means as you read and study this emotional story.

■ Getting Into the Word

Hosea 1–3

Thoughtfully read through Hosea 1–3 twice. As you read, think about the following questions:

1. One question that students of Hosea have had is whether the story of Hosea, Gomer and their children is literal or figurative. Are the events described in these chapters literally happening, or are they a parable? On the basis of your reading, what would you say? What are your reasons?

2. Hosea 1:2 reads, "Go take to yourself an adulterous wife and children of unfaithfulness." Was Gomer an adulterous woman, or a prostitute, when Hosea married her, or did she become one later? Did God truly command Hosea to marry such a woman, or is Hosea describing Gomer as he looks back on his experience? Your answer will depend, to some extent, on how you read the rest of the story and how you understand the history of Israel. Since the experience of Israel is compared to that of Hosea and Gomer, how do you see Israel? Was Israel originally "pure" when God "married" her, or was she always "adulterous"? Read and compare Ezekiel 20:1-13 and Jeremiah 2:2, 3. How do you harmonize these two passages?

3. What are the names of Gomer's three children? Using the Bible text and a Bible dictionary, find out the meaning of these names. How does each fit with the story of Israel? Hosea 1:10–2:1 and 2:22, 23 speak of these names being changed in the future. How are the names changed, and what are their new meanings? What do these name changes mean for Israel?

4. Make a list of the misconceptions and false ideas that unfaithful Israel has about her "lovers" as given in chapter 2. What does she think they will do for her in return for her "favors"? What steps will God take to "educate" her and

teach her the wrongness of her ideas and the inability of her lovers to really care for her?

5. God not only wants to teach Israel, He also wants to bring her back to Him. List the steps God uses to bring Israel back. When she comes back, what will life be like? How will it be different?

6. What did it cost Hosea emotionally to love Gomer again? There was an actual financial cost to get Gomer back. What was the cost? You can find these answers in Hosea 3. Using a Bible dictionary, find out the monetary value of a shekel of silver and an homer and a lethek of barley (3:2). How does this cost compare with the usual cost of a slave? What does this say about Gomer's condition?

■ Exploring the Word

Marrying a Prostitute

Because the description of Hosea's family life is so brief, unique, and provocative, widespread discussion has arisen concerning its exact nature. There is little question about the basic teaching of Hosea and the general way God uses the story to teach Israel. On the other hand, many interpretations exist as to precisely what happened in Hosea's life.

Two major questions must be answered. First, is the tale of Hosea's family life something that literally happened, or is it merely figurative, a parable? The second question concerns Gomer and her children, the time frame of the story, and whether or not she really was a prostitute. We will discuss these two questions in order.

The account of Hosea's family life seems to be literal, not figurative or allegorized. At first reading, the accounts of Gomer seem like an actual episode rather than a symbolic tale. Although the names of the children have clear symbolic meanings and the story is told specifically because Israel is guilty of spiritual adultery in her departure from God, several other things point to the literal nature of the story. For example, the names of Gomer and Diblaim seem to be simply names without any allegorical meaning.

Also, how do you "figuratively" take a wife? If Hosea did not really marry Gomer, then we have something allegorical symbolizing something that is also allegorical. Yet the usual rule of analogy is that something *literal* points to something symbolic. The symbolic meaning of Israel's idolatry and waywardness is clear. It makes sense that something literal should lie behind it rather than something allegorical.

Further, the power of the book lies in the poignancy and pathos of Hosea's experience. Much of that impact is lost if the story of Hosea and Gomer is not literally true.

David Hubbard suggests that this story is not an allegory, but enacted prophecy (Hubbard, *Hosea*, 52). Hosea "speaks" for God not only through his words, but through his personal life. Hosea himself is a sermon, even if he says nothing. As we feel and experience with Hosea, we begin to understand the heart of God with all its pain. Hosea teaches us not merely the thinking mind of God, but the feeling heart of Yahweh. As we sense what all this cost Hosea, we get a glimpse of the price God paid to keep on loving Israel.

The second question, concerning the nature of the adultery Gomer was involved in and the time frame of the story, is not so easily answered. Numerous explanations have been given, but almost all of them fit into one of three basic interpretations.

The most common interpretation is called the "proleptic" view (see, for example, McComiskey 1:11-15 and Hubbard, *Hosea*, 54, 55). This viewpoint understands Hosea 1:2 as being written from a later time frame, projecting back into the story what actually happened at a later time. In this view, Gomer was not an adulteress or prostitute when God commanded Hosea to marry her. She was an Israelite woman who only later proved to be unfaithful. This understanding of the story takes the "children of unfaithfulness" in 1:2 as reading later realities back into the text. Thus the children of 1:2 and 1:3-9 are one and the same group of offspring.

This proleptic view requires a particular understanding of Israel's history. If Gomer started out pure, then Israel should also be seen as a pure bride during her time as a fledgling nation. Three passages in

Hosea appear at first glance to describe Israel's history in this way: 2:14-16, 9:10, and 11:1-4.

One of the main arguments for this view is that God never would have commanded Hosea to marry someone who was already immoral. That would have been unthinkable and wrong. Besides, Hosea never would have considered doing such a thing.

The second major explanation is that the marriage of Hosea and Gomer is literal, but Gomer's "adultery" is not. Since all Israel had strayed from God and was participating in "harlotry," this included Gomer and her children. Gomer engaged in some aspects of the ever-present Baal worship and was (or became) in this way a prostitute (Stuart, 26, 27). This understanding gets God off the hook of commanding marriage to a literal prostitute. Various linguistic arguments have been used to support this understanding (Stuart, 26, 27).

The third major explanation takes Gomer's prostitution literally and believes that Hosea took her as a wife from that situation. Some Bible students also believe that God's command, "take to yourself . . . children of unfaithfulness" (1:2), means that Hosea was to adopt the children that Gomer bore as a result of her promiscuity (McComisky, 15-17). This would mean that Hosea had two groups of children—those God commanded him to take, who had been born to Gomer while she was a prostitute, and those Gomer bore to Hosea after their marriage (Hosea 1:3-9).

The strength of this third viewpoint is that it seems to be the most natural reading of the text. Some versions alter the time frame to suit their proleptic view—such as the new RSV, that adds the word *have* before *children* in 1:2. The fact remains that this third explanation seems to take the actual Bible text most seriously.

The major objections to this third viewpoint are theological and historical. Theologically, some simply cannot see God actually commanding such a thing. But I ask, how is this any worse than the proleptic viewpoint? According to that interpretation, Gomer may not yet have been an immoral woman when God instructed Hosea to marry her. But does that fact resolve the problem if God knew beforehand that she was going to turn out to be a prostitute? And doesn't God invite us to "marry" Him even though we have been, and may be at present, "adulterers" in sin?

As for the historical objection, the picture is not that clear. While some texts seem to point to a pure time in Israel's history, I am convinced, having just studied the book of Exodus, that it is hard to argue for some earlier period of Israelite history that was "pure" and "holy." This is especially true in the light of Exodus 32:1-10 where in the very midst of enacting the covenant—the marriage—Israel commits spiritual adultery by worshiping the golden calf!

Others have argued against this literal view from the standpoint of ethics. Marriage to harlots, they say, was forbidden. In actual fact, the Pentateuch prohibited marriage to a harlot only on the part of priests (Lev. 21:7). In no passage is one who was not a priest—and Hosea is not portrayed as one—forbidden to marry a harlot.

As you can see, I tend to favor the literal explanation of God's command to Hosea to marry an adulterous wife, although I think good reasons can be given for the other two views. I like interpretations that take the text seriously, even though they may raise questions. This literal view does that.

I also like theological implications of this view for our understanding of grace. God did *not* pick Israel and "marry" her because she was a wonderful, pure bride. He chose her while she was a sinning slave simply because He was gracious and loving and wanted to keep His promise. If Hosea's experience is meant to be a mirror in which we can see God, then it makes sense that he is to show the same amazing grace as God does. That means taking a sinful bride. As the prophet was literally commanded to take an immoral, unfaithful woman as his wife and adopt her (not his) children, so God takes sinful people in all their ugliness as His wife and children. Our state is never so bad that Yahweh refuses to stop wooing us, marrying us, and taking us back.

Gomer's Three Children

Following the title to Hosea in 1:1 and the command to marry Gomer and Hosea's obedience in verses 2, 3, God discusses Gomer's three children in 1:4–2:1. There we find brief statements about their births and the names of the two sons and one daughter, followed by an application to the condition of Israel.

This passage clearly illustrates a pattern that follows throughout the book of Hosea that is also common in other prophetic books. Statements of judgment and doom alternate with sayings of hope and restoration. Hosea 1:4-9 is a section of judgment sayings, while 1:10–2:1 portrays hope. The verses in 2:2-14 tell of future punishment, while verses 14-23 ring with a voice of hope.

What Hosea 1:4-9 states about the three children refers to judgment. The very meaning of their names tells of the punishment of Israel. Most people in western culture think little about the literal meaning of the names they give their children. Boys named Jake or Jacob and girls with the feminine form of the name, Jacqueline or Jackie rarely know that their name means "liar" or "deceiver." Names are given on the basis of pleasant sound or in honor of a beloved relative or friend. On the other hand, Hebrew names were usually given with the meaning of the name or a historical reference in mind. This is certainly true of Hosea's children, who are named not by their parents but by God Himself.

The first son is named Jezreel (1:4, 5). Literally, the word can mean "God sows" or "God scatters," since scattering seeds was the usual method of sowing. In this passage, the name seems to have a double meaning. The first is the literal one—God scatters. God will scatter Israel in judgment.

This interpretation is altered, however, in Hosea 1:11. Hosea 1:10–2:1 is a restoration passage. The children's names, which in the preceding judgment passage are used to symbolize the tragedies to come, are here reversed by God to symbolize hope and restoration. In 1:11 Judah and Israel are "reunited," have "one leader," and come up out of the land of exile. The restoration passage in 2:22, 23 declares that God will again "sow" or "plant" His people. The earlier "scattering" is reversed as people are brought together and "planted" in the land.

The second meaning of Jezreel's name is its identification with the earlier tragic history of Israel. At Jezreel, Jehu had killed the kings of Israel and Judah in cold blood. Jehu had also slain everyone connected with the house of Ahab. Thus the city was connected in the Israelite mind with violence and murder (see 2 Kings 9, 10). Jezreel's name is a symbol that God will punish the house of Jehu and put an end to Israel. Her "bow" (1:5), i.e., military power, will be broken. To name a child Jezreel was like calling a child today "Auschwitz" or "Hiroshima" or "My Lai"—all places of violence and death (Limburg, 9).

The second child born to Gomer is a daughter. God declares that her name is to be "Lo-Ruhamah," which means "not loved" (1:6). This daughter and her name are to illustrate that God will no longer show love to the northern kingdom of Israel.

In Hebrew the prefix "lo" is the negative—"not" or "no." In the restoration passages of 2:1 and 2:23, God removes the *lo* from her name. She becomes Ruhamah, "My loved one." Her younger brother has been called Lo-Ammi, meaning "Not my people," referring in judgment terms to Israel (1:9). The *lo* is also removed from his name in the salvation passages, and "Lo-Ammi" becomes "Ammi," meaning "My people" (2:1-23). Thus God is able to change judgment into mercy and restoration as He changes the names of Gomer's children.

These three names portray a horrible progression of judgment. First, Israel is to live without king or nation. Second, her future is one without God's love. Third, she is no longer God's people, and He ceases to be her God. Then, just as amazingly, God changes the names, and the horrible progression is reversed! Israel becomes a nation and has a leader (1:11); she again becomes God's loved one and His people (vss. 1-23).

No other prophet has such a close link between his prophetic calling and personal life as does Hosea. His wife and children are directly and intentionally a part of His ministry. Hosea never was able to leave his message and work "at the office."

After people knew Hosea's family and message, his preaching could be done without words. He could preach a powerful sermon just by introducing his family and letting the people see them. Every place they went they were walking, talking, real-life videos with a message. Certainly no one could accuse Hosea of not feeling his message personally!

Israel's and Gomer's Problems

The passage in Hosea 2:2-23 is written in poetic, prophetic verse form in contrast to 1:1–2:1 and 3:1-5, which are in prose, narrative form as they tell Hosea's story. Hosea 2:2-23 attempts to expand in detail what God means by the statement that the "land is guilty of the vilest adultery" (1:2). In another sense, the whole passage attempts to answer the question of why a terrible judgment has been foretold. What is God's reason for doing this? The section reads like a lawsuit or legal accusation in which Yahweh lays out His case against Israel as a prosecutor would put forth the case against an accused criminal. Although there are clear allusions to Gomer, Hosea, and their children in the passage, it is basically God speaking to wayward Israel.

The message is that Israel must cease being unfaithful to Yahweh, or she will be "stripped naked" (lose her land, wealth, and resources) and be turned into a parched desert (2:3). Israel (and Gomer as well) has not just received lovers who came to her. She has actually gone out looking for paramours. The reason is that she believes they are the ones who give her food and water. Israel holds that these false gods have provided her with wool, linen, oil, and drink (vs. 5).

The meaning in the life of Israel is clear. Israel has been accepting the worship of Baal and the Canaanite gods and participating in the fertility rites connected with them. She has been deceived into believing that her food, drink, and clothes are gifts of Baal, so she has pursued him in order to obtain these things.

The Canaanites believed in what is sometimes called imitative magic. This concept teaches that nature imitates what humans do. In order to make their animals and land productive and fertile, the Canaanites practiced religious prostitution and immorality. When humans performed acts meant to produce children, nature followed in imitation. Animals had babies, and the land produced crops. These immoral acts were believed to be both religious and necessary to making a good living in agriculture.

Hosea tells Israel that she needs to understand how mistaken she is. Baal is not the source of these things—Yahweh is (vss. 8, 9). The way God will teach Israel proper theology is to take away what she has enjoyed (vss. 9-13). Her abundant harvests and plentiful herds must be taken away. Her clothing must be stripped off. Only as she loses these things will she realize where good things really originate.

God's Amazing Grace

God, however, is not interested simply in punishment. Hosea 2:14-23 switches gears and talks of how God will restore what is lost. Note all the good things God proposes to do for His "bride":

1. God will court Israel with tender words (2:14).
2. God will give back her vineyards (vs. 15).
3. God will restore hope and song (vs. 15).
4. God will become her husband, not just her lover or paramour (vs. 16). In this verse, the first word used for a male is the usual word for "husband." The second word (*my master*, NIV) is literally "Baal," which is the word for a Canaanite god and also the word used for a male lover or paramour.
5. God will remove the Baal names from her lips (vs. 17).
6. God will make a new covenant (marriage) with her and all nature (vs. 18).
7. God will abolish war and battle and make the land safe (vs. 18).
8. God and Israel will be married forever in love, justice, and faithfulness (vs. 19).
9. Israel will acknowledge God as her God (vss. 20, 23).
10. The land will again be productive (vss. 21, 22).
11. God will plant Israel in the land (vs. 23).
12. God will love Israel and call her "My people" (vs. 23).

I have listed these things to vividly impress on our minds the goodness and graciousness of God. Yahweh makes all of these wonderful and amazing promises while Israel is literally a spiritual harlot far from God! It is like a multi-billionaire marrying an immoral prostitute and promising her his estate. No specific repentance is called for. No specific conditions are laid down. God wants to restore His wayward people, and He will do so. What marvelous and amazing love and grace!

Taking Gomer Back

In Hosea 3:1-5 we return to Hosea's personal life for the final play in the drama. The Lord comes to the prophet and commands, "Go, show your love to your wife again, though she is loved by another and is an adulteress" (vs. 1).

Although some interpreters claimed that this refers to a woman other than Gomer, most believe this passage refers to her, even though her name is not mentioned. It would seem strange to introduce a new woman without naming her. The symbolism of the story would seem to be destroyed as well. Hosea and Gomer are a parable of Yahweh and Israel; to introduce another party would wreak havoc on this meaning. The word *again* in verse 1 seems to tie this story to the earlier saga of Gomer.

A threefold pattern emerges in this passage: (1) command, (2) action, then (3) interpretation (Stuart, 63, 64). The first sequence, however, reverses the order of the last two elements. Using this pattern, the passage would look something like this:

Command: (God to Hosea) Show your love to your wayward
                wife again (vs. 1a).
Interpretation: This parallels how God loves the adulterous Israel
                (vs. 1b).
Action: Hosea buys Gomer back (vs. 2).
Command: (Hosea to Gomer) Refrain from any sexual intimacy
                (vs. 3).
Interpretation: Israel will live in oppression without government
                or organized religion (vs. 4).
Action: Israel's chastening leads to a return to God (vs. 5).

While chapters 1 and 2 talk in bold outline of judgment and restoration, this section introduces a new element. Although God will "buy" Israel back, there will be a period of discipline during which God's people will be without many things. This will lead to a later time when she comes to herself and recognizes her condition and seeks God and His blessings.

As always, this experience parallels that of Hosea. When Gomer returns to Hosea, she is to refrain from her promiscuity and not sleep even with Hosea. Her deprivation (and Hosea's) are to symbolize the temporary separation of Israel and God. This means that the NIV marginal reading of 3:3b, "I will wait for you," is correct, while the textual reading, "I will live with you," is incorrect.

Oh, how we wish more details were available! What has happened between chapter 1 and 3? How and why did Gomer leave Hosea? If they were married, why does he have to *buy* her back? What happens after this? Do they now live happily ever after?

On most of these issues we can make only some educated guesses. In some way or another, Gomer is enslaved by another party—possibly her lover. Quite possibly Gomer experienced debt slavery, which was common in those days. People who borrowed and could not pay what they owed were the property of their lender. As an adulteress, Gomer could have been driven out of Hosea's home with nothing and been forced to borrow.

The money that Hosea pays for Gomer (3:2) seems to be the usual price for a slave. Exodus 21:32 puts the price of a female slave at thirty shekels of silver. Although Hosea only pays fifteen shekels of silver, the barley (about thirty bundles) is probably worth about the same as fifteen shekels. It is difficult, due to differing economies, to calculate precisely what the price Hosea pays is worth in modern terms. The fact that there is a mixture of items may mean that Hosea had to scrounge to get enough money to buy Gomer back.

We don't know what happened to Hosea and Gomer after the price was paid and after the period of separation. In some ways, the simple, barebones story we have evokes more emotion than if we had all the juicy details. We are moved to think about the anguish and heartache involved, and in our minds we can paint many possible concluding scenarios.

A good title for this section would be, "The Tale of Four Loves."

Hosea 3:1 uses the Hebrew word for "love" four times. Each time the meaning differs, and each meaning is instructional to us. Two of the types of love are counterproductive and evil. Two are powerful tools for good.

The first of the evil loves is the love of the immoral paramour. Hosea's wife is loved by another. This love is a burning, passionate attachment to that which is not ours. The love is an adulterous craving which seeks to satisfy self and does not hesitate to ignore and trample on the commitment made in the marriage covenant.

The second destructive love is the love of the sacred raisin cakes. These cakes were used in the worship of other gods. This is a love that has fallen prey to the allure of the happiness, joy, and fun promised by false religion. This love forgets the goodness of God and goes for what seems pleasant in the present.

As for the two positive, powerful loves, the first is Hosea's love for Gomer. This love is a love based on principled response to God's command. This love is founded on an imitation of God's love because Hosea is called to do only what God has done already in His relationship to Israel.

The second positive, changeless love is Yahweh's love for His people Israel. This love is not based on how the object of love responds. Rather, it comes in spite of what the beloved does! This love keeps on loving because it is faithful to its promises—unlike the first two evil kinds of love.

In reality, these four kinds of love define the message of the book of Hosea. The clear call is to flee from the false loves of the paramour and the raisin cakes. These loves destroy and are like mirages that appear wonderful to the eye but on closer examination prove false and temporary. The call is to respond and follow the two true loves. Even though it will involve anguish and pain, it is the only way to salvation, peace, and lasting hope.

It becomes abundantly clear that what God does and what He calls Hosea to do is painful. It is not easy to take an unfaithful woman for a wife, later to buy her back, love her, and then for a period of time not be intimate. The evil of Gomer and Israel punishes Hosea and Yahweh! Other parts of Scripture clearly speak about what God does and says. Hosea, more than any other book, shows how God *feels*. In other parts of the Bible, God bares His powerful right arm in action; He bares His mind as He reveals His thoughts. But here in Hosea, He bares His *heart* so we can sense how He feels. Not only that, His faithful message bearer, Hosea, cannot stay separate and detached. He also becomes part of the story in an intimate way. As the two suffer together the anguish of steadfast love, they draw us into their circle and invite us to do the same.

■ Applying the Word

Hosea 1–3

1. Do any particular names of people or places signify either judgment or salvation to me? What are they, and what do they mean? If I were to give myself a name signifying the meaning of my life, what would it be? What name do I think God would give me? Why?

2. If I were to compare my life with God to a marriage, how would I describe the relationship as it is today? Courtship? Honeymoon? Married folks growing old together? On the rocks? Separated? Verge of divorce? In counseling? Why? Have I ever left God or cheated on Him? How? How can I get back together with God if I am unfaithful?

3. Have I ever attributed blessings I received to "Baal"? Have I ever forgotten what God has done for me? What other lovers have I chased after because I wanted to get something from them? What are these "Baals" for me today?

4. What kind of love predominates in my life? Love of a paramour? The raisin cakes of pleasure? Love for others? What does love mean for me? How closely does my love parallel that of God?

5. Could I take back an adulterous spouse? What would be the prerequisites? How would I feel about doing this? What does this book teach me about marriage?

6. How do I think Hosea felt about God and His prophetic

call? How would I respond to such a call? Would I like to work for God if He made such a strong demand on me? What does this tell me about the call of God?

■ Researching the Word

1. Using a concordance and looking under the words *adultery* and/or *harlotry* find all the places that the word is used in a spiritual sense of Israel's unfaithfulness. Is it used as much in this sense as it is in the literal sense? Why do you think this usage is so common? What does this teach us about Yahweh's relationship with Israel? What should this teach us about how God looks at unfaithfulness?
2. Hosea 3:4 speaks of four specific things Israel will be without in her worship practices during the period of her separation from Yahweh. Two of the four are valid parts of Yahweh worship—"sacrifice" and "ephod." Two are associated with Baal worship—"sacred stones" and "idol." In reality, these latter two items are special words which have quite specific meaning. Using a Bible dictionary and/or a Bible commentary, find out what these words actually mean. How are these things used in Baal worship? Why do you think they are mentioned here? What does this tell us about worship in the northern kingdom in Hosea's time?

■ Further Study of the Word

1. For general insights, see E. G. White, *Prophets and Kings*, 279-292.
2. For an introduction to the worship practices of Hosea's day, see King, *Amos, Hosea, Micah*, 88-107.
3. For an exposition of suffering in the book of Hosea, see Fiddes, "The Cross of Hosea Revisited," 175-189.

CHAPTER THREE

A Wayward Israel

Hosea 4–10

The story of Hosea's family life is finished. We can begin to sense how God feels about Israel because we have felt the agony of His prophet. Now we must look in detail at the precise situation of the Israelite nation. We have seen, in general, how God looks at her position. Now it is time to look at the fine points.

Hosea 4–10 is a series of somewhat loosely organized poetic prophecies about Israel. Their main thrust is to point out exactly what Israel has done that is wrong and what God plans to do in response. The picture is not a pretty one. Hosea minces no words in his vivid descriptions. The situation is desperate, and it would do no good to minimize the problems.

These seven chapters can be divided into three major sections. Hosea 4:1-3 lays out the basic central charges against Israel. The passage in 4:4– 7:16 speaks to the sins of the nation's leadership and of their judgment. They bear special guilt because of the duties entrusted to them. The final section, chapters 8–10, address the punishment that will fall on the nation at large.

■ Getting Into the Word

Hosea 4–10

Read Hosea 4–10 twice. On the second reading, begin to answer the following questions:

1. Hosea 4:1-3 outlines the basic charge against Israel. Study this passage carefully. List the three basic things that God does *not* find in the land. What does this say about God's central concerns? What are the sinful practices that follow on the heels of the general wrong attitudes found in vs. 1?

2. Religious leaders have an important place in the statements Hosea makes about judgment. List all the statements that Hosea makes about the priests in chapters 4, 5, and 6. Why do you think the priests are singled out?

3. The royal house and other governmental rulers are also singled out for judgment. Read carefully chapters 5, 6, and 7, and list all the statements that specifically speak to the king, the royal house, princes, and rulers. What are their particular sins? Why are they mentioned?

4. As you read this section of Hosea, try to specifically define spiritual adultery. List all the religious practices that are specifically mentioned that God despises or that are called harlotry or adultery. Hosea emphasizes this kind of religious sin, and we can learn from his explanations. What stands out in your mind as you read these passages?

5. Notice all the passages that mention Assyria. Write down all these statements, and ask yourself what role Assyria had in Israel's future. How would an Israelite feel after hearing all these statements about Assyria?

6. Hosea 8–10 talks about the punishment that will come on Israel. List the specifics of this punishment. Does it sound harsh? What overall picture do you get of God after you read this? Of Israel? Why does God have to keep "pouring it on"?

■ Exploring the Word

Lacking the Basics

Hosea 4:1-3 portrays a courtroom scene. The wayward Israelites are called to listen to a formal court indictment that lays out the situation in which they find themselves. The Lord "has a charge to bring against them" (vs. 1). This charge is the framework for the details that follow.

This basic charge states that three things are missing among the Israelites—"faithfulness," "love," and "acknowledgement of God" (vs. 1b). These three words represent major concepts in the Old Testament and deserve a closer look. Understanding these words will help us understand that the accusations against Israel are not over minor, nit-picky issues but touch the core of Israelite faith.

The word translated "faithfulness" ('emeth) is in other places often translated "truth." The Hebrew word occurs 126 times in the Old Testament and is a core value of the Bible. 'Emeth is of such high worth that everyone should seek it (Proverbs 23:23). The word is often combined with the second term in this list, "love" (hesed). These two words may be the most basic description of what the people of God should be like.

Probably the closest English word to the root meaning of 'emeth is "reliability." The person who is "faithful" or "true" in his words and actions is practicing this virtue. A person who has 'emeth in his innermost being is truly reliable in character and action. Such reliability is manifested in personal relationships and is not simply an objective, abstract truth. Unfortunately, this basic trait is missing in Israel.

The second thing lacking in Israel is "love," or hesed. In the Old Testament, hesed is not the only word translated "love." In fact, another word, 'ahab, is used more often to refer to that idea, and hesed is often translated as kindness. Hesed occurs 245 times in the Old Testament. It implies mutuality. Those who have received hesed from another are expected to show the same to every other person. It is natural, then, for hesed to be connected with the covenant. Since a covenant establishes a mutual relationship, hesed is a way of being loyal to a covenant.

Three basic elements are part of the concept of hesed. It is active, social, and enduring. Hesed is not just an idea, but a practice of kindness and loyalty to a covenant partner. Since it is performed on behalf of another in a relationship, it is a social concept, not an individual one. Real hesed lasts because we do not, or should not, forget our covenant relationships.

This word is especially important in Hosea because the accusation is that Israel has forgotten her relationship with Yahweh and her obligations as a covenant (marriage) partner. God has shown *hesed* to her and deserves it in return. Its lack in Israel is appalling. It is like a child who has forgotten the *hesed* of a parent, or a spouse who has forgotten the marriage vow. This is sin at the very core of one's being.

The third thing that God says is not existent in Israel is an "acknowledgment" (*da'at*) of God (4:1b). The verb root of the word *da'at* ("knowledge") is used more than a thousand times in the Old Testament and ninety times in the specific noun form we find here.

The NIV translation "acknowledge" seems to miss the mark. In Hebrew, the verb "to know" refers not so much to intellectual or abstract knowledge as it does to personal, intimate, experiential knowledge. While the cognitive is not absent, the emphasis is on the affective realm. To have no knowledge of God implies a failure to have a personal relationship with Him

In Hosea, the absence or lack of knowledge parallels the word "forget." Israel theoretically knows about God and what is right— at least to a degree—but she has conveniently forgotten and acts as if she didn't know. Hosea 4:6 makes this plain. Since Israel has forgotten ("ignored," NIV) the law of God, Yahweh will forget her children. Tragically Israel has chosen to put aside, forget, ignore, etc., what she theoretically knows and thus lives as if God weren't there.

Lacking these three basic attitudes or life orientations is tragic. They are the root cause for all of Israel's problems. Out of this lack comes all the specific sin problems—cursing, lying, murder, stealing, and adultery—mentioned in verse 2. All bonds are broken, and bloodshed follows.

These specific sins are all covered by the Ten Commandments. When the basics are wrong, the details are also wrong. In looking at the situation in our world today, I wonder if we don't often deal with the details or specifics rather than the basics. When we have crime in our streets and bloodshed in our cities, we put more police on the streets and give longer prison sentences. What has become of the basics of "faithfulness," "love," and "knowledge"? How do we teach people these life orientations? If they were in people's hearts, the specific problems would disappear.

As a result of Israel's problems—both general and specific—judgment comes. The judgment mentioned in 4:3 sounds almost ecological. The land "mourns," and its dwellers waste away. Beasts, birds, and fish die.

This result teaches us a profound lesson. In the mind of the Old Testament, all of life was part of a seamless whole. Theological sins such as a lack of faithfulness and love lead to problems in the physical environment. Israel's sin affects all nature. Problems in nature are a tip-off that something is wrong elsewhere.

This insight is still true. Do not sins such as arrogance, irreverence, selfishness, and greed help lead to environmental problems even today? If we really cared about others and thought of future generations, would we not walk softer on the earth that God has created?

Problems With Priests, Prophets, and Civil Leaders

Hosea 4:4–7:16 emphasizes the leadership of Israel. Both religious and civil leaders bear special responsibility for the disastrous situation in which Israel finds herself. The people have gone astray, and faulty leadership is a key reason this has happened.

The accusation begins with the religious leaders. Priests are specifically mentioned six times in chapters 4 to 6 (4:5, 6, 7, 9; 5:1; 6:9). Hosea 4:5 also seems to mention the prophets (false ones) in the same way. This makes sense because priests and prophets in the Jerusalem temple served the cult together (see Isa. 28:7; Jer. 2:8; 4:9; 5:31; 6:13; 8:10; 14:18; 18:18; 23:11; Micah 3:11).

The meaning of the initial verse in this section (4:4) is not clear in the NIV. Verses 5 and 6 speak of direct judgment on the priests. Verse 4 probably refers to the same thing and should read something like:

> Yet let no one make a complaint,
> And let no one reprove,
> For my complaint is against you, O priest
> (Limburg, 19).

If this is the case, the whole section (4:4-6) makes sense as a direct indictment by God of the priests and prophets. The rest of the chapter deals indirectly with the priests. Their sins and the accompanying results are spelled out in detail, and then they are specifically addressed again in 5:1.

What is the problem with the priests? They have failed to give the people knowledge. The people whom God has given them to teach are "destroyed from the lack of knowledge" (4:6). This lack of knowledge comes because the priests have "ignored the law" of their God (vs. 6). Law in this case could also be translated as "instruction." The priests have failed to perform their God-given function—instructing the people about the will of God.

The passage speaks as directly as any in the Old Testament to the awesome responsibility that religious leaders have to teach people. For Israel proper, religious teaching—theological education—is not just a nice option. It is literally a matter of life and death. People are not simply left ignorant by this lack of knowledge—they are destroyed. The punishment for this clearly falls on both priest and people (vs. 9).

What follows in chapter 4 and on into chapter 5 is a detailed description of where this lack of knowledge has led. Israel is specifically accused of using the cult and sacrifice to get food (4:7-10), practice divination (vs. 12), offer sacrifices at high places (vs. 13a), participate in ritual sex orgies (vss. 13b, 14), encourage drunken lewdness in connection with false worship (vss. 17-19), promote false trust in pagan sacrifices (5:6), and give birth to bastard children from pagan orgies (vs. 7). The clear idea is that lacking real knowledge of the true God, they have gotten involved in the local false religion, and a whirlwind (4:19) will sweep them away.

This passage embodies not so much a general topic to preach or teach about to all people, as it does a special word for preachers, teachers, and religious leaders. Their task is a heavy and important

one. Transmitting the knowledge of God can make or break a church
and/or a nation. Leaders must take their jobs seriously.

This knowledge of God has at least four dimensions (compare
with Limburg, 21, 22):

1. *Relational or Experiential.* We must not forget that this is the
book of Hosea and that the Yahweh/Israel relationship is like the
husband/wife marriage bond. That bond is based on personal, intimate, experiential knowledge. The Hebrew word *yada'*, "to know,"
can be used of the sexual union between husband and wife (see, for
example, Gen. 4:1, KJV). To have a knowledge of God is to have a
real, personal encounter with Him.

2. *Covenantal.* Israel and Yahweh were united by a covenant. Covenants had legal implications. There were regulations, stipulations,
and conditions connected with a covenant. Part of a knowledge of
God is to understand not only the covenant, but the good results
(blessings) of keeping it and the bad results (curses) of breaking it.
Hosea and Yahweh are appalled at the adulterous covenant-break-
ing that Israel indulges in.

3. *Cognitive.* Part of knowledge is knowing the facts. The theolo-
gian must teach the actual happenings that make up the story of
God's actions for His people. What God has done and is doing and
what He asks of His people is an essential part of knowledge.

In Hosea, the priests seem to have this cognitive part of knowledge themselves, but they have refused to practice it or pass it on.
They have "rejected knowledge" (4:6).

4. *Commitment.* The final and most crucial part of knowledge is
that it must be acted on. People who cognitively know about God
still need a commitment to follow what their theoretical knowledge
tells them is true. True knowledge includes instruction that a decision of the will is part of the package.

Today, anyone who bears a responsibility to teach or preach about
God must understand and convey all four areas of knowledge. Simple
cognitive teaching is not enough. All dimensions of knowledge should
be portrayed as part of the package if we want to save people from
the destruction that comes upon those who lack knowledge.

Hosea is not satisfied simply with dealing with Israel's religious leaders. The civil and governmental leaders also bear blame for Israel's plight. The royal house itself is involved in the sin that has brought Israel to the point of downfall (5:1).

What is it that the rulers have done? Hosea's indictment of the rulers is not as clear as is his indictment of the priests. Hosea seems to be dealing with the priests first in this section (vss. 4-7). However, beginning in verse 8 he appears to be dealing with the governmental leaders. This section, after many twists and turns, ends with the statement in 7:16 that the rulers will fall by the sword.

Israel is condemned for the political ups and downs of its relationship with Judah, the southern kingdom (5:8–6:11a). Also under scrutiny and judgment is its vacillation between Assyria and Egypt. Israel was always wondering which of the two it should ally itself with (5:13; 7:8-16). Finally, the palace intrigue with royal instability clearly manifest themselves (6:11b–7:7). Government and politics are obviously a mess. Crime is rampant in the streets, but people still don't realize that Yahweh remembers (7:1, 2).

One of the reasons it is hard to tell in detail who and what is being condemned is the fact that we know so little of the history of the period. For some suggestions regarding the broad lines of historical events mirrored in this section, see a good commentary of Hosea (for example, Hubbard, *Hosea*, 118-120).

In broad outlines, we see a nation that is in chaos. The people have apostatized and abandoned God. Priests and religious leaders are corrupt. Government is also literally falling apart. Weak, vacillating, and indecisive rulers come and go with great speed. Crime is prevalent. It is only a matter of time before everything collapses. Hosea would say that this is a result of sin and Israel's abandonment of loyalty to Yahweh. Spiritual adultery lies behind all this.

What Is Spiritual Adultery?

What is spiritual adultery or religious prostitution? Why is it called this? Why is it so prevalent in Hosea? What can we learn from this? As you read this section of Hosea, especially chapters 4 and 5, the numerous references to adultery or prostitution certainly must jump out. Some form of the word prostitute or prostitution occurs eight times in chapter 4 alone. This concept is important to Hosea.

It is no coincidence that the use of this word occurs in the sections of Hosea that emphasize the sins of the priests and the religious apostasy of the people. Prostitution and adultery refer specifically to the spiritual/religious sins of the people. When the Lord is not acknowledged as God, then some other master must be found. Because God is Israel's husband, to abandon Him for some other god is adultery. To receive material gain for this unfaithfulness becomes prostitution. Israel is like a woman of easy virtue who sells her allegiance to whomever will "pay" (or bless) her.

This comparison is even more appropriate when you realize that the god Israel chose to serve was usually Baal. The word *baal* is actually a title that means "lord," "master," and even "husband" but later became the proper name of the most worshiped male deity in Canaan.

Baal was a fertility god. According to the mythology of the cult, Baal died annually. This was proven by the summer drought and winter kill seen in nature. When Baal "died," he descended into the underworld for a period. While there, Baal found his mate, usually a female goddess such as Anath or Astarte, and they mated. As a result of this sexual union, nature came alive again. Rain came, crops grew, and livestock multiplied.

Canaanites believed in imitative magic. People imitated the gods, and the gods imitated people. As part of worship in the "high places" and groves, male worshipers would enter into a sexual relationship with a woman who was usually a cult prostitute. They would imitate Baal, then expect Baal to imitate them and make the earth fruitful. They were thus seen as helping to resurrect nature and restore fertility to crops and animals. Worshipers of Baal saw such practices as vital to the continued prosperity of their land. This was literally a vital part of Canaanite farming and animal husbandry.

This blatant sexual immorality in the name of religion makes the terms *adultery* and *prostitution* even more appropriate. One can also see why such acts are referred to as "prostitution." The favors (blessings) supposedly gained by these acts led to farming success for the year. Many Israelites probably fell into Baal worship as they learned agriculture from the Canaanites.

Looking back at the Israelites from our perspective, we are often very hard on them. We are amazed at their readiness to abandon the worship of Yahweh and follow Baal. Careful thought, however, could lead us to see that there were attractive aspects to Baal worship, and it certainly promised certain benefits.

Baalism furnished a religious rationale for a form of free sex. You could enjoy yourself sexually, feel religious, as well as believe you were helping productivity. All this had a powerful allure.

The fertility cult was relevant to the daily life of people. Most Israelites were farmers and/or herdsmen, and the worship of Baal spoke to their needs. It provided a way to work for fertility of land and livestock. People felt that their religion was crucial to their economic success.

Baal worship offered pleasant occasions in nature. Sacrifices were offered on mountaintops with a variety of trees where "the shade is pleasant" (4:13). People could get away from the daily grind and go to a pleasant place for worship and relaxation.

This false worship also allowed Israelites to enter into pleasant relationships with the local Canaanites. By adopting some of the local religious practices, social and economic relationships with the Canaanites were easier. In some areas, the Canaanites may have even been higher on the social ladder than Israelites, and adoption of their practices meant social prestige.

The danger of false religion is that it always *seems* good. It appears to make sense. The same is true today. Modern baals are no different from ancient ones. They appear to be just what we need—and fun as well! It takes discernment to realize the terrible end they lead to.

This is the very reason the knowledge we talked about earlier is so crucial. Only when people have an adequate knowledge of the true God can they clearly see the differences between false and true religion. Israel's priests have a solemn duty to make the right path clear.

In Hosea the real problem is not just her rejection of Yahweh, but her religious compromise. Israel did not so much desire to throw Yahweh away as to have Baal also. That, of course, is the nature of adultery. The very word implies that a person is married, but has someone else on the side. Israel desired to remain wedded to Yahweh but wanted to have an affair with Baal! You can almost hear Israel say to Yahweh, "Be reasonable; I'll give you your due worship, but I'd like to spend some time with Baal, also."

The thrust of the book of Hosea, and of the whole Bible, is that this combination of Yahweh and Baal worship is completely unacceptable. When Hosea is reconciled with Gomer in Hosea 3, she is to live with Hosea alone (3:3). She cannot be intimate with any other man. Israel cannot live with any other man either. To do so meant "divorce" from Yahweh and the terrible judgments that Hosea outlines.

Hosea's desperate burden is to have Israel recognize where she stands. She is utterly guilty of religious adultery. Her religious leaders have failed to instruct her and bear special blame. Because of this terrible sin, she stands under judgment. Exactly what that judgment means is the subject of our next section.

Assyria and Judgment to Come

The two major powers outside Israel that figure in our story are Assyria and Egypt. Although these two nations lie behind all the six books covered in this volume, Hosea mentions both by name much more frequently than any of the other five prophets. Their presence is clearly in his mind as he writes. Because Assyria is the power that eventually takes the northern kingdom captive, we will deal mostly with her.

Chapters 4–10 of Hosea names Assyria five times (5:13; 7:11; 8:9; 9:3; and 10:6). Israel is like a senseless and easily deceived dove (7:11). To turn to Assyria for help is foolish, for she cannot cure Israel's problems (5:13). In fact, to go to Assyria is also a form of prostitution—political prostitution (8:9). The end result will be the payment of tribute to Assyria and finally be in captivity there (9:3; 10:6).

These passages make it clear that, first of all, Israel should have feared Assyria and stayed away from her. If Assyria could not help Israel and would, in the end, capture her, why go to her?

Secondly, consorting with Assyria was committing that horrible sin of adultery. It was condemned in its religious form but is now denounced in its political form. Adultery involves the death penalty, and Israel would do well to steer clear.

The fact of the matter is that Israel doesn't seem to hear and/or obey. If she persists, as she seems to be doing, punishment will result. Spiritual and political adultery bring the same results. Hosea 8–10 spells out in detail what some of those results are.

The most basic punishment seems to be captivity by a foreign nation—Assyria in this case. Hosea 8 opens with the words, "Put the trumpet to your lips! An eagle is over the house of the Lord." The trumpet is most likely the trumpet of alarm (see also 5:8), which the prophet is to blow. The eagle or vulture is Assyria. This enemy will pursue Israel (8:3).

Over and over, the same theme occurs. Israel will be "swallowed up" (vs. 8) and will suffer oppression under a mighty king (vs. 10). The nation will "return to Egypt" (vs. 13), i.e., to slavery in a foreign land. Israel will not "remain in the Lord's land," but will "eat unclean food in Assyria" (9:3). God's people will be "wanderers among the nations" (vs. 17).

Everything the people love, cherish, and enjoy will be lost. This includes their false religious idols and high places (8:6; 10:2; 10:5, 6; 10:8), their cities and towns (8:14; 10:14), their children and offspring (9:11-14, 16), and their king (10:7, 15). Crops and food will fail (9:1, 2). Yahweh even goes so far as to say He will no longer love them (vs. 15).

Why does God seem to be "pouring it on?" Why don't one or two statements suffice? Why must people be told over and over that they will be taken captive?

Hosea is, of course, not unique in this regard. Old Testament prophetic books have a habit of pounding long and hard on their favorite topic of judgment. That is one of their trademarks. What can we say about it?

First, we need to remember that the prophetic books are, in most cases, compilations of prophetic statement. As such, these judgment statements represent the sermons of the prophets over an extended period of time. Judgment statements are grouped together and represent the long-term work of the prophet.

Second, the proclamation of judgment was the basic work of the prophet. Prophets who talked of good things to come were specifically the prophets who needed to be tested (Jer. 6:13, 14; 8:10-12). The prophets' God-given work was to call for reform, and that involved clearly spelling out the results of continued rebellion. The call of God seems, at least in some cases, to be so strong that the prophets could not help themselves even if they wanted to (Jer. 20:7-9).

The repetition is also, I believe, related to human nature. Unless we hear something repeatedly, it often has little effect on us. Judgment is urgent and crucial. The people must reform, or they are lost. When you feel that something is really important, you must emphasize it.

Hosea 4–10 is Hosea's desperate call to Israel to recognize the seriousness of her situation. She has committed spiritual and political adultery, and the result will be destruction and the loss of all she holds dear. In these chapters, the thought of judgment is hardly relieved by any mention of hope. Israel must listen if she expects to survive.

But is there any hope? The answer is "Yes," but we must wait until the next chapter to hear it. For Hosea, like most prophets, the order is first judgment, and then hope. God judges that He may truly heal in the end. This we will discover in our next chapter.

■ Applying the Word

Hosea 4–10

1. **If God were to take our contemporary society to court, what would His indictment be? Would it, like Israel's, be that we are lacking faithfulness, love, and acknowledgment of God? Or would it be something else? What are the basic things**

we lack before God? What are the root causes of our religious problems?

2. Do our sins in the religious realm affect society and the physical environment? If so, how? Why? Is it right to divorce religious belief from social sins? Why, or why not? If they are connected, what does this say about how we should view life and politics?

3. Do you think the quality of religious leadership is as important today as it was for Hosea? Why, or why not? What effect do our religious leaders have on us? How can we help them do their job well?

4. If God were to speak to "priests" today, what would He say? Who would the priests be? Would He condemn them or praise them? Do priests today "ignore the law"? How? What can we do about it?

5. Do God's people today lack knowledge? What kind of knowledge? What type of knowledge of God is most crucial today? Why? How can we help people get the right knowledge?

6. What is spiritual adultery today? Is it attractive? Why? What can we do to help those who are involved in spiritual adultery? Would we use the same terminology as Hosea does? Is there a modern equivalent to Baal worship? What would it be?

7. Do we need to speak judgment to people today? Why? How can judgment be spoken of so people really hear what is being said? Could we do it the same way as Hosea? Why? Should there be people today like Hosea? What would they be like?

■ Researching the Word

1. Hosea mentions a number of cities or towns in this section of his book. Understanding where these towns are and what role they have in history helps to make the text come alive. Using a Bible dictionary and a Bible atlas or the maps in a

Bible or Bible dictionary, look up these towns. Based on what you find, try to determine why Hosea mentions them.
2. Many commentators see the Syro-Ephraimite war as a general background to this section of Hosea. Read about this war in 2 Kings 16:1-9 (2 Chron. 28:5-7). Read Isaiah 7:1–8:22, which also alludes to the conflict. Do you agree with those who say that this war is a background to the book of Hosea? What are the reasons for your answer?

■ Further Study of the Word

1. For general insight, see E. G. White, *Prophets and Kings*, 293-300.
2. For further information on Baalism and Canaanite religion, see a good Bible dictionary, and look under the heading of "Baal," "Asherah," "Canaan and religions of."
3. In Hosea 10:1 Israel is compared to a vine. In this connection, read Deuteronomy 32:32, Psalm 80:8-11, Isaiah 5:1, Jeremiah 2:21, and a good Bible dictionary under the heading of "vine." What is the meaning and significance of calling Israel a vine?

CHAPTER FOUR

A Loving Lord

Hosea 11–14

This section begins with a refreshing change. After the war, violence and turmoil of Hosea 4–10, Hosea recalls Israel's early days when she was a "child" (11:1). Like a parent reminiscing to a mature youth about the love, joy, and tenderness that were bestowed on the child in an earlier time, God recalls His love for Israel. That early love still exists and continues to influence the way God treats Israel even now. Like a small amount of good perfume can sweeten the atmosphere of an entire room, so chapter 11 makes the whole book of Hosea exude a special aroma that would not be there if the chapter were absent.

Hosea has not forgotten, however, that Israel now lives deep in sin. In chapters 12 and 13, he renews his prophetic proclamation of judgment. Israel is lying and deceitful. As such, she deserves and will receive the judgment of God. There is, however, hope. If Israel decides to return to God and asks Him to forgive her iniquity, He will heal Israel's wounds and restore her.

The typical "first doom, then hope" cycle of the prophets continues, and the book ends in chapter 14 with the final word that there is a chance, even now, for God's people to return to Him and be saved.

■ Getting Into the Word

Hosea 11–14

Read Hosea 11–14 through thoughtfully twice, and then answer the following questions:

1. Hosea uses various forms of the Hebrew verb, "love," nineteen times. (Contrast this with Amos and Micah, who use the word only twice.) Various other related Hebrew words are also translated into English as *love* in some versions. Love is thus an important concept in Hosea. Look for the places where the word *love* occurs in this section of Hosea. Note especially 11:1, 4 and 14:4. In a paragraph or two, discuss why love is so important in Hosea and what the word seems to mean.

2. Although God is not directly called "Father" in this passage, many statements are made that assume He is like a father or parent. An example would be when He calls Israel "My son" in 11:1. Make a list of all the statements that clearly imply God is like a mother or a father. What do these statements tell us about God?

3. Look at Hosea 11:1 carefully. Who is Israel? What does it mean when God says "out of Egypt have I called My son?" Does the verse sound like a prophecy or more like a statement of history? Matthew 2:15 quotes part of this verse. Matthew states that Jesus fulfilled it when He came out of Egypt where His parents took Him to escape Herod. Does Matthew really understand the meaning of Hosea 11:1? Is he using the passage correctly?

4. This whole section is full of references to events and people in Israel's past that reach back even into patriarchal times. It is hard to understand what is going on here unless one recognizes what events in this period of history are referred to. Beginning with 9:10, make a list of biblical events and people that are mentioned. What is the purpose of all this? Is this a valid use of history?

5. Hosea contains many powerful images of God. In the early parts of the book, He is often presented as a loving, faithful husband. In Hosea 11 (and other places as well) He is a caring Father. What is God compared to in 13:7-9 (see also 11:4.)? What special insights can you learn from these images of God?

6. **In chapter 14, Israel is called to return to God. When she does so, she is to acknowledge specific things before God. Make a list of these things (14:2, 3). Also make a list of what God promises to do in response (14:4-8). How does 14:9, the last verse of the book, fit with all of this? How is chapter 14 a fitting conclusion to the book?**

∎ Exploring the Word

God Speaks of His Love

Hosea 11:1-11 (11:12 in English is actually 12:1 in the Hebrew text and starts the next section of the book) is a moving passage about God's enduring love and care for Israel. There seems to be no direct tie between this passage and what goes before and after it. Condemnation and destruction frame this section at the beginning and the end. It is as if both the prophet and the Spirit have decided that in the midst of all this judgment there must be a statement about love.

The entire passage is divine speech. God Himself talks directly to His people. Even though verse 10 talks *about* God in the third person, verse 11 returns to the first person and portrays the whole section as being spoken by the Lord. Such use of different pronouns is quite typical of the Hebrews, and they would not have been bothered by it. God's expression of love comes from His own mouth.

God's love is portrayed over three time periods: 1) Israel's past (11:1-4); 2) Israel's present and immediate future (11:5-7); 3) Israel's distant future (11:8-11). We will deal with each of these in turn.

In the past when Israel was a young nation, "a child," God brought His "son" out of Egypt. The reference in 11:1 clearly is talking about the Exodus from Egyptian slavery. This is evidenced by the statement in Exodus 4:22, 23 in which Israel is called Yahweh's "firstborn son" and Pharaoh is told "Let my son go. . . ." The Exodus liberation is especially the time when God uses sonship language with Israel. Hosea follows that lead.

The Exodus deliverance is the basic salvation event in the Old

Testament. That event is a mighty demonstration of God's love. Paraphrasing 11:1 would result in something like this: "When the Israelites were a little people and helpless, I loved them like a parent loves their child. As a result of that love, and as a demonstration of it, I delivered them and set them free from Egyptian slavery."

Although in this passage Israel is referred to as "my son" (11:1) or "sons" (vs. 10, RSV), Yahweh is never directly referred to as "Father" or "Mother." Parenthood is implied but not stated. In nine Old Testament passages, God is expressly called Father (see, for example, Deut. 32:6; Jer. 3:19; 31:9). Other passages clearly present maternal images of a God who as a mother quiets a child at her breast (Ps. 131; Isa. 49:15). The portrayal of God in Hosea 11 is not clearly maternal or paternal. Both parents love their child (vs. 1). Both can teach a son to walk, hold him in their arms, and heal him (vs. 3); both are needed to bend down and feed him (vs. 4). The Bible portrays God as *both* mother and father. Although father is used more often, God is bigger than human gender, and Bible writers use both male and female comparisons to show His greatness and goodness, depending on the situation and the audience.

The tragedy of Israel's past is that in the face of that deep parental love, Israel was a very wayward child who not only strayed, but rebelled and followed idols—false parents. She came to the place where she seemed to not even know what the true Parent had done for her (vs. 3).

What is this "love" that Israel rejected? At least two clear meanings are implied in the Hebrew word for love, *'ahab.* The first meaning is one common to those influenced by western culture—a deep affection. Yahweh cares a great deal for Israel. He actually seems to be fond of her.

Second, love is related to covenant faithfulness (see Deut. 6:5-9; 7:8). Both God's love for Israel and Israel's love for God imply a willingness to keep promises that have been made. God is loyal to Israel. Like a parent who never abandons his child even when he disappoints, God stays by His son, Israel. This He does in spite of the fact that the child leaves Him.

What about the situation in Hosea's day (11:5-7)? Has the rebellious "child" changed? Emphatically, No! Israel still refuses to return to God (vs. 5b) and is bent on turning away (vs. 7a).

As a result, Israel must go back to the land of "Egypt" (vs. 5). Egypt in this case is clearly a symbol for the land of the conquering enemy. As Israel was once in bondage in literal Egypt, she will return to slavery in a new "Egypt." That new Egypt is literally Assyria. Returning to Egypt and having Assyria as "king" is an example of synonymous parallelism, which is common in Hebrew poetry. The two sentences are just two ways of saying the same thing. "The swords" (vs. 6a), meaning war, will ravage Israel's cities and fortresses. Israel will fall into slavery, and worse yet, "none shall remove it" (vs. 7, RSV). Hope seems to be gone.

Then Hosea switches gears in verse 8. The tragic picture of a perpetually enslaved son is more than a loving parent can bear. God is appalled by His own words, as appropriate as they may be in the situation. He finds He cannot really give up His son Israel (or Ephraim) for all time. His heart and love will not allow it! So we have a surprise verdict. In the end, God will *not* let Israel be lost forever. As He looks to the third time period—the distant future—God sees a restored Israel.

Several details of this restoration are interesting to examine. Admah and Zeboim are two cities on the plain that were obliterated along with Sodom and Gomorrah (Gen. 10:19; 14:2-8). The covenant curses in Deuteronomy 29:23 specifically mention these four cities as examples of what would happen to Israel if she strayed from the covenant. God is saying He has trouble doing to Israel what He has promised. He can't utterly destroy His "son," because His very nature will not allow it.

Yahweh will not *again* destroy Ephraim. The little word, *again*, in verse 9 (RSV) is crucial. The salvation God is offering the northern kingdom is not escape from destruction by Assyria in 722 B.C. That is the first destruction, which in this passage seems inevitable. God is promising a process of renewal and salvation that begins *after* that. Those who survive the catastrophe need not fear a coming calamity. This should also have given some hope to righteous Israelites in Hosea's day.

A key element in this promised restoration is Israel's response. Chapter 11:10 begins with the words, "They shall go after the Lord." A repentant people decides to follow Yahweh. Only then are they able to see their punishment come to an end.

The summons to return comes from Yahweh's lionlike roar. Hebrew has four different words for "lion." Hosea 5:14 and 13:7, 8 utilize two different words for lion when they use the word in a negative sense for Yahweh's destroying work. Hosea 11:10 uses a different word which is the most common term for the king of beasts. The great, maned African lion is referred to here as it is in other places in the prophets where it carries a more positive connotation (see Amos 1:2; 3:8; Joel 3:1b). The roar of the lion seems to be a clarion call for all people to hear God's judgment or decision (Stuart, 182). In this case it seems that God has decided Israel is to be restored.

The positive lion's roar brings God's children back. They fly in like birds from all over—the west, Egypt, and Assyria (11:10, 11). Rather than trembling (as the NIV, KJV, and RSV translate it), they are returning *hurriedly* or *speedily* (TEV, NEB, JB). The Hebrew word used can be translated either way, but "speed" or "hurry" makes more sense in this passage. God has decided that Israel is to be restored to her proper home. He has roared it to the world, so why should there be delay? Like birds on the wing, Israel hastily flies home to rest in her ancestral land.

The whole story of Hosea 11 is one of various returns. The Hebrew word *shub* can mean "turn," "return," or "repent." Four different returns are mentioned in the passage:

1. Israel's sin causes her return to "Egypt" (vs. 5a).

2. That return has come because Israel won't return to Yahweh (vs. 5b).

3. Israel turns away from God in apostasy (vs. 7).

4. Finally, in spite of all Israel's problems, Yahweh returns Israel to her home (vs. 11).

In the end, that is the real story of divine love. In spite of all our wrong turns and returns, the final word always belongs to God. He causes our return home. That part of Hosea's message is always true.

Hosea and Messianic Prophecy

This is a good place to raise the question about messianic prophecy in Hosea. We have just examined in depth the teaching of Hosea 11:1-11 and endeavored to explain its meaning. Hosea 11:1b, "out of Egypt I called my son," is quoted in Matthew 2:15 and applied to the flight of Joseph and Mary into Egypt with the infant Jesus. Matthew specifically states of the flight to Egypt, "so was fulfilled what the Lord had said through the prophet." Our examination of 11:1 in its original context, however, found that the passage clearly refers to Israel's Exodus from Egypt. What is going on? If our explanation of chapter 11 is correct, how can Matthew be right? Hosea 11:1 doesn't really sound like a prophecy of the future, because both its verbs are actually in the past tense and seem to refer to Israel's history—not her future.

The answer lies in understanding what Matthew is trying to do. Matthew tries to show in his Gospel that Jesus fulfills all the hopes and dreams (and prophecies) concerning Israel. He wants to bring Jews to faith in Jesus. One of the ways he does this is to see the history of the Israelite nation, God's sons (children), recapitulated in the life of Jesus (God's special Son). Just as Israel started with the miraculous birth of a son (Isaac), so the new Israel, the church, began with the miraculous birth of a Son (Jesus). In line with this general idea, Matthew 2:15 is trying to say that as the "son" nation of Israel ended up in Egypt yet was eventually brought out, so was the Son Jesus. Jesus relives Israel's history.

Some will ask: Can, or should, Christians use the same principles of Bible interpretation today? My answer is, "It depends." I believe God led Matthew to apply Hosea 11:1 this way because this kind of interpretation was well known to both Matthew and his audience. It communicated well. Both Matthew and his readers' faith in Jesus fulfills all that God was working toward with His people Israel. In some cultures people still see Scripture in these ways. For them, this is a valid way of using Scripture.

On the other hand, many in our twentieth-century world, with its emphasis on history and science, have trouble with this kind of methodology. To such people, Matthew's way of using the Old Testament seems artificial. For them, these interpretation methods are counterproductive. They do not communicate. There are, however, many other ways that can be used to lead people to believe in Jesus. A good missionary or evangelist uses the method that most clearly communicates with the way his audience thinks and evaluates truth. The basic need, however, is that Bible interpreters understand Matthew's mind and methodology so that their own views of how prophecy should operate don't warp their interpretation of Exodus or Matthew and lead to problems.

Hosea and Israelite History

One characteristic of Hosea is his extensive use of references to Israel's earlier history. Some of these references occur prior to the section of Hosea that we are examining in this chapter. Where are all these verses? What do they mean, and what can they teach us?

Note the following passages:

"When I found Israel, it was like finding grapes in the desert . . . but when they came to Baal Peor, they consecrated themselves to that shameful idol and became as vile as the thing they loved" (Hosea 9:10).

"Since the days of Gibeah, you have sinned, O Israel, and there you have remained. Did not war overtake the evildoers in Gibeah?" (Hosea 10:9; cf. 9:9).

Hosea 11:1-4 which we have just studied talks about God's love for Israel and her later sin of following the Baals.

"In the womb he [Jacob] grasped his brother's heel; as a man he struggled with God. . . . He found him at Bethel and talked with him there" (12:3, 4).

"I am the Lord your God, who brought you out of Egypt;

I will make you live in tents again, as in the days of your appointed feasts" (12:9).

"Jacob fled to the country of Aram; Israel served to get a wife, and to pay for her he tended sheep. The Lord used a prophet to bring Israel up from Egypt" (12:12, 13).

"I am the Lord your God, who brought you out of Egypt. . . . I cared for you in the desert, . . . when they were satisfied, they became proud; then they forgot me" (13:4-6).

"So in my anger I gave you a king, and in my wrath I took him away" (13:11).

The importance of looking back at Israel's history becomes clear when you realize that the verses quoted above are just the major sections of Hosea that specifically refer to Israel's history. Other minor references, referring to various geographical places, also occur. Much of the rest of this section of Hosea is an explanation of the meaning Hosea sees in these historical references. For Hosea, Israel's history was a fertile ground to draw on in making the points he felt necessary to bring Israel back to God.

What Hosea does is use "then and now" arguments. What happened "then," i.e., Israel's historical situations, explains the "now," the present plight of God's people. In most cases, the idea is that at one time things were good. When God met Israel in the desert, it was like the discovery of some wonderful grapes (Hosea 9:10). Israel was loved (11:1) and cared for (13:5).

In a very short time things took a bad turn. Israel sinned at Baal Peor (9:10; see also Num. 25) and Gibeah (9:9, 10:9; see also Judg. 19–21) and by idol worship (13:1). She forgot God (vs. 6) and didn't recognize Him as her Healer (11:3). The results of that sin continue on to the very present. History is the basis for God's indictment of Israel. She knew better and was once better. She had lost her way *not* because God failed to tell her or instruct her, but by her own sinful choice.

In the earlier section of this part of Hosea's book, most of the historical references seem to be specific *places* and *events*, but in the latter part of the section, references seem to be to *people*, particularly Jacob, and to their *characteristics*. God seems to be looking at particular feelings, attitudes, and relationships that people have. We must remember that the history of God's people can still be used today to teach us things we must know in the present. Such a practice has a long illustrious history that goes back to the Old Testament.

God's Healing Path

The last chapter of Hosea is a clear message and moving portrayal of how Israel can emerge from the judgment and punishment which result from her sin. As a final appeal, Hosea tells what the path back looks like. Israel needs to know where she is now, but as a last word, she must also discover what things can be like in the future if she decides to return to God. The chapter is also a wonderful model for today. Those who may wonder what the way back to God would look like can learn here. We can all profit from a close look at the wonderful passage that points out the path of healing.

The chapter falls into three major sections. Verses 1-3 tell Israel what a proper approach to God in repentance would look like. Verses 4-8 portray what God's response would be if Israel follows this approach. Verse 9 concludes with an appeal to follow God's way.

How can Israel get out of the terrible situation in which she finds herself? Hosea's simple answer is, "Return to the Lord" (14:1a, 2a). This appeal is not new in the book of Hosea (see especially 11:5; 12:6), but this final chapter makes clear its centrality. To take this very literal Hebrew word, *shub*, which means "turn" or "return" and translate it as repentance is to lose something very important. Repentance in English often implies sorrow for some action. To read 14:1 as "repent, O Israel, to the Lord your God" misses some of the meaning. To keep the literal translation is better. Israel must not so much feel sorrow for something, but rather, turn away from sin and the Baals and return to righteousness and *God*. This is a personal appeal. God was affronted as a husband and lover by an Israel that has run after the Baals. Israel's need to is return to *her* God.

To make this return, Israel must recognize that her sins have caused her problems (vs. 1b) and *take words* with her to speak to the Lord as she returns to Him (vs. 2a). Sacrifices will not do. A relationship has been severed, and the only way to repair it is to come with the right words.

What are the right words? They contain three requests, three admissions, and one conclusion.

Request one: "Forgive all our sins" (vs. 2). As all sins are forgiven, the path is open to do other things.

Request two: "Receive us graciously" (vs. 2). Forgiveness paves the way for God to receive the sinner. That reception is recognized as gracious. God does not have some obligation to do this—He does it because He is full of grace.

Request three: Enable us to "offer the fruit of our lips" (vs. 2b). Here words are compared to sacrifices of animals or produce. The words offered seem to be the people's promises to keep God's covenant and worship Him. If God forgives and receives Israel, He should also accept their "offering" of words that pledge to follow Him.

Following these three requests that Israel should make to God are certain key admissions. These confessions or admissions relate to acts she has done in the past and how wrongheaded they were.

Admission one: "Assyria cannot save us" (vs. 3). One of the major problems in Hosea is reliance on foreign powers. Israel must admit that this is wrong and renounce foreign entanglements.

Admission two: "We will not mount war-horses" (vs. 3). Israel had begun to depend on military might, and that implied horses and chariots. This was in direct opposition to Deuteronomy 17:16 (see also Ps. 33:17). Usually Israel depended on Egypt for its horses, so war-horses not only fostered a false trust in military power, but foreign dependence as well.

Admission three: "We will never again say 'Our gods' to what our own hands have made" (14:3). Probably this is the most important admission of all. Reliance on foreign powers and military

might was wrong, but not as galling as idolatry. Israel's worship
of foreign gods and the belief that they, rather than Yahweh, were
the source of blessing was appalling. Israel must surely admit and
forsake this sin.

The conclusion to all this is the recognition that all the requests and
admissions are based on an assumption about God's nature—He is
compassionate (vs. 3b)! Even the fatherless, who have no legal rights,
find compassion with Him. If Israel can remember God's compassion, then she should have the courage to go ahead with the requests
and admissions found here.

The big question is: "If she does all this, how will God respond?"
What will He do? Hosea 14:4-8 gives the answer.

The marvelous answer is that God promises "I will heal their
waywardness and love them freely" (vs. 4). God will be both their
Healer, or Physician, and their Lover, or Husband. He who once
wounded them will now heal, and He who once divorced them will
marry them. That is good news.

The following verses, which detail what this healing and loving
will be like, sound much as though they come from the biblical book,
Song of Solomon. That wonderful book of love poems is filled with
the same lush nature imagery that we find here. The talk of dew (vs.
5), blossoms (vss. 5, 7), fragrance (vs. 6), and cedar and pine (vss. 6,
7, 8) all evoke that place of love. God places in the minds of people
the image of a marriage of two people in love. This book, which has
so much of the agony of a broken love relationship, returns at the
end to the glories of married love. The love relationship that Israel
has ruptured will be restored by God. Israel and Yahweh will honeymoon again and revel in the joy of conjugal love.

After this powerful presentation of hope for the future, Hosea makes
his final appeal in verse 9. This call for decision is based on the Old
Testament "two ways" doctrine. There is a right way and a wrong way.
A wise way and a foolish one. The Lord's way and our way. As Proverbs
appeals to the reader to choose the wise way, Hosea does the same thing.
In the light of all this, "Be wise!" he says. The Lord's way is the right
one, so walk in it! I'm sure that appeal applies as much today as it did
then. Please, reader, choose the wise way and live.

■ Applying the Word

Hosea 11–14

1. This final section of Hosea talks about God's love. In particular, chapter 11 portrays Him as a caring Parent. Do I believe God has been a loving Parent to me? How has my belief been shaped? Does God seem more like a father or a mother to me? How can *I* see God as a nurturing Parent when so much punishment and judgment is found in Hosea? How do these different acts of God fit together?

2. What principles do I use when I interpret Scripture? Are there certain ways that are not valid? Why, or why not? Would it be right for me to use the same principles Matthew did with Hosea? How do I go about applying the principles found in Hosea to my time and place?

3. What does my life history in relationship to God look like? Have there been times when I was close to God? When are/ were they? Have there been times when I strayed? Why? As I look at my history, what does it mean? What does it teach me? How can I view my history so it can benefit my walk with God?

4. Love is a word we use often, but its meaning varies greatly. This chapter has tried to explain some of what Hosea's definition of love is. What is my definition of true love—especially God's love to me? How has Hosea's explanation of love helped me understand love? How has my understanding of love been influenced by what Hosea teaches?

5. Do any of my problems trace their origin back to my straying from God? The three sins Israel specifically confessed in Hosea 14 are trust in and alliance with foreign powers, faith in military might, and idolatry. Have I trusted in "foreign" powers, had faith in something other than God, or put various "idols" alongside God? Could it be that the path to healing that Hosea gives in chapter 14 could apply to me? How?

6. The book of Hosea is meant to show us how Gomer's and Israel's waywardness bring pain and agony to Hosea and God.

What do I see in the world, the church, and my life that
brings agony to God and His ministers today? If God asked
me to write a book that showed His hurt in today's world,
what would it be like? What would it talk about?

7. Many people today feel the church needs renewal. What can
I learn about the principles of renewal for God's people from
Hosea? How can I know when renewal is needed? If it is
needed, how does it come about? What message should be
preached to people who need renewal?

■ Researching the Word

1. Matthew uses other Old Testament prophetic passages in
his book besides Hosea 11:1. Some of the main ones are
Matthew 1:22, 23 (Isa. 7:14); Matthew 2:17, 18 (Jer. 31:15);
Matthew 4:14-16 (Isa. 9:1, 2); and Matthew 12:17-21 (Isa.
42:1-4). Look at the passages carefully, and check a Bible
commentary if you have one. Does Matthew use the same
principle(s) of interpretation in all these passages? Does he
use these passages in the same way he does Hosea 11:1?
What can you learn from this?

2. Israel, according to Hosea, should confess her sin of dependence on *war-horses* (Hosea 14:3). Find out what you can
about the role horses played in war. Scan a concordance on
the words "horses" and "war-horses," and read those texts
that talk about the use of horses in war or the problem of
trusting in horses. Compare your findings with what you
discover in a Bible dictionary or encyclopedia's articles on
"horses" and "war." What new insights does this give you
on why God forbade Israel to have such horses (Deut. 17:16)?

■ Further Study of the Word

1. Hosea (chapter 14 in particular) refers to many animals and
plants found in Israel. To find out more about them, look
up the plant and animal names in your Bible dictionary, or

see P. King's *Archaeological Commentary*, and read chapter 5, which is on agriculture, plants, and animals.

2. We have finished our study of Hosea. One way to fix the book in memory is to review its basic contents. D. Kidner's *Message of Hosea* gives a good bird's-eye synopsis on pages 137-142, or you can read a good Bible dictionary under the heading "Hosea."

PART TWO

Joel

Facing the
Day of the Lord

CHAPTER FIVE

Introduction
to Joel

Joel writes as God's crisis management expert. Something terrible is in the process of happening to Judah. Her land stands devastated by what the prophet calls "locusts." Destruction reigns everywhere, and drought threatens. Into this moment of crisis steps Joel with warnings and answers.

The prophet tells us what happened. He proclaims what the immediate response of God's people should be. He explains what Judahites should feel in their hearts. Most importantly, Joel talks about the future and hope. The terrible situation now is not the end. God's final answer then involves restoration and blessing. Any human facing crisis today can learn from these ancient words of wisdom.

■ Getting Into the Word

To begin to understand Joel's overall message, read the book through in one sitting—there are only three chapters. As you read, look for answers to the following questions:

1. Try to understand as clearly as you can what is happening in Judah. Do the locusts seem real? Why? What else happens as a result of the "locusts"? What crisis does the nation face?
2. What response does God want from His people? What should Israel be doing to meet the crisis she faces? How will these responses help solve the problem?

Joel the Man

Joel's name means "Yahweh is God." He cannot, however, be identified with any of the other twelve figures in the Old Testament who
bear the same name. His father, Pethuel, is also unknown. The only
other Bible book where Joel is mentioned by name is Acts (2:16),
where his book is quoted.

From a reading of the book itself, we can glean certain facts about
this prophet:

1. He comes from the southern kingdom of Judah. Jerusalem and Judah
are mentioned in the book, and the northern kingdom of Israel is
not spoken of. Neither is its capital, Samaria.

2. He is a good writer. Although his book is short, it is well-written.
The poetry shows careful crafting and word choice. The book uses
apt and persuasive arguments, and the language conveys powerful
emotions and vivid images. The style is sublime and elevated.

3. He is familiar with the temple and its services. A major discussion
in scholarship today is the relationship between the prophets and
the temple.

Some have suggested that Israel had prophets connected specifically with the temple—prophets who ministered in the temple ritual
services. They are often called cult prophets. Whatever the case,
Joel clearly understood and was interested in what happened at the
temple. He may have been a priest as well as a prophet.

Historical Setting

Probably no prophetic book is harder to date than Joel. Most
prophets mention at least one king by name. Joel fails to do this. In
fact, the whole book contains no name or any event that can be clearly
dated. Babylon and Assyria—the two crucial enemies of God's
people—are not mentioned either.

Because of these facts scholars are not sure how to date the book.
Proposals range from the ninth century B.C. (800s), or early pre-
exile period, to the post-exile period 400 years later. Most arguments
used to date the book are based on silence; i.e., what the book does

not say more than what it does state.

The good news is that the dating of the book does not really affect its message. Whatever date is chosen, the basic teaching of the book still applies. My personal preference is to date the book in the early 700s or late 600s B.C. My reason is the order of the books in the Bible. I think they were placed roughly in chronological order, which means the time frame for the book is between Hosea and Amos.

Theme and Message

I have chosen to subtitle Joel's book, "Facing the Day of the Lord." For Joel, the crisis Israel faced in the locust plague and its resulting devastation was met by an understanding of the day of the Lord. That "day" is the theme of his book.

The prophet sees this "day" as not a single, literal day, but as at least two occasions. The coming of the locusts themselves was in some sense a "day of the Lord." The locusts are God's army and perform His will (2:11).

The other "day of the Lord" comes "afterward" at some later time (vs. 28). What happens at this later day of the Lord is not the same thing that took place at the first one. While the initial day of the Lord was mostly bad news, this later day of the Lord is good news of hope and restoration. In fact, the book is divided into two parts each of which talk about one phase of the day of the Lord.

Joel is important particularly to Christians because of Peter's quote from the book in Acts 2:17-21 during his sermon on the day of Pentecost. Peter sees the coming of the Holy Spirit in Acts 2 as the fulfillment of this second, later day of the Lord as foretold by Joel.

I think what Joel would say today is that whatever crisis we face—however horrible it may be—the answer lies in the day of the Lord. That day is the time when God comes near to right wrongs and to do His work to save. As long as we can believe in a coming "day of the Lord," there is hope.

Outline of Joel
Facing the Day of the Lord

I. Facing the Locust Day of the Lord and Judgment (1:1–2:17)
  A. Title (1:1)
  B. The locust invasion and a call to mourning (1:2-20)
  C. The locust army and a call to return (2:1-17)
II. Facing the Future Day of the Lord and Salvation (2:18–3:21)
  A. God delivers His people (2:18-32)
  B. God judges the nation (3:1-21)

CHAPTER SIX

Facing the
Day of the Lord

Joel 1–3

Since the short book of Joel will be covered in one chapter, the Introduction to the book which you have just read serves as introduction to this chapter. You may want to quickly reread it with that thought in mind.

■ Getting Into the Word

Joel 1–3

Read through the book of Joel again thoughtfully. As you read, answer the following questions.

1. One of the major questions about the book of Joel is the nature of the locusts. Many Bible students believe the plague of locusts to be referring to literal locusts. Others argue that the locusts are only a symbol of a military invasion. Which of these views is correct? What is the evidence from the Bible itself? State your answer, and then make a list of the texts and reasons that you would give to support your answer.
2. As we have stated in the Introduction, the major theme of Joel is the "day of the Lord." The phrase occurs in 1:15; 2:1, 11, 31; and 3:14. Look at these texts, and make a list of all the things that are to happen on or around the day of the Lord. On the basis of this list, formulate a short definition of what you think the day of the Lord really is. What do you

think would be a good short phrase that could be used as a synonym for the phrase "day of the Lord"?

3. There are many interesting time references in Joel, but you will need to read carefully to notice them. Some of the more important ones are "near" (1:15; 3:14), "close at hand" (2:1), "now" (vs. 12), "then" (2:18; 3:17), "afterward" (2:28), "in those days and at that time" (3:1), "in that day" (vs. 18). What do these time references do for us? After studying them, what can you learn about the time sequence of Joel?

4. Acts 2:17-21 quotes Joel 2:28-32a. After reading Joel, go to Acts and compare the two passages. Do you notice any differences? What are they? Why are they there? What is the difference between how Acts and Joel use this information? What does this teach you about the Bible's use of other Bible passages?

5. Part of God's restoration of Israel is a judgment on the foreign nations. Analyze Joel 3, and then list all the nations or cities that God names to receive judgment. Also list the reasons God gives for the judgment that comes. Is God fair in what He does? Why, or why not? What does this teach us about God's dealing with the nations?

6. Events connected with the locust plague and the final day of the Lord call for responses from God's people. Joel doesn't leave that response up to the whim of the people. He specifically calls for certain responses. List the various kinds of responses Joel calls for. Do these responses vary with different groups of people? Why, or why not? What can this teach us about what God wants from us?

■ Exploring the Word

The Locust Plague

With only a single, short sentence of eight terse Hebrew words, Joel introduces his book. He wants people to know that what he says is Yahweh's revelation to him—"The word of the Lord that came to

Joel" (1:1). As a good Hebrew, he must also name his father, so due respect is given, and family ties are recognized. Beyond these short basics, all that matters is the message that is clearly urgent. No historic references or mention of kings is given or needed. To get to the message quickly seems to be his aim.

What Joel is concerned about is locusts (1:4; 2:25). What this plague of winged insects has done is clearly outlined in 1:5–2:11. The devastation is horrible and affects every area of life.

For years people have debated over the nature of these locusts. Today most believe that Joel is talking about literal locusts, although a significant minority hold that the locusts are a figurative description of a military invasion that Judah suffered. Fortunately, the basic message of Joel is not seriously affected whichever view one holds. My basic position is that the locusts are literal. (For an argument on the opposing side, see Stuart, 241, 242.) Some of the reasons for my views are the following:

1. The general description given seems to fit a real locust plague. The major emphasis seems to be on the devastation the locusts bring to nature. Fields are ruined (1:10); grain is destroyed (vss. 10, 11); fruit crops suffer (vs. 12); and even livestock suffer from loss of food (vss. 18, 20). While such things could happen in war, a more likely description would include loss of human and animal life and the destruction of cities.

It is true that these locusts are called an army (2:2, 11) and compared to warriors (vs. 7), but even then the description ends up sounding like real locusts. This "army" darkens the sky (vs. 2). This army leaps over mountains (vs. 5). The battle force scales walls (vs. 7) and runs along them (vs. 9), rather then breaking them down like soldiers would do. They enter windows like thieves (vs. 9). All of this sounds more like literal locusts than the attack of an army of men.

2. The specific descriptions of the locusts are quite detailed. Joel knew what locusts really were like. Joel 1:4 uses four different terms for locusts out of nine possible Old Testament words. The exact meanings of these words are not known, and English translations vary in how they translate the words. Some have suggested that the words represent four stages of the locust life cycle (Watts, 16). If this is so, the first stage is the larva, or grub, stage. Following the grub stage would be a nymph stage, where no flying is done, but the locust is a crawling devourer. The third stage is the swarming stage in which the locusts develop wings and prepare to fly to new areas in search of food. The last stage is the mature insect. The process of this development can take as much as three years.

Even if these different words do not clearly depict the life cycle of locusts, it would seem strange to use so many different technical words for locusts if they were only a general symbol for something else. Even the passage that talks of God's restoration of Israel from the effects of these locusts uses a number of different specific terms to describe them (2:25).

We should not leave the subject of locusts without trying to sense how horrible a plague of locusts can be. It is obvious that what happened in this plague greatly impressed Joel. Nothing like this, he believes, has happened in the lifetime of the elders of Israel or in the days of their forefathers (1:2). Israelite children are to be told of it, and they are, in turn, to pass the word on to their children who will tell the next generation. This is big news.

Nowadays locust outbreaks can be prevented in many cases. Careful monitoring can spot incipient locust swarms, and they can be destroyed by pesticides. In earlier times such things were not available.

When locusts enter their gregarious swarming stages, they can migrate great distances. They have been observed 1,200 miles out at sea. The total size of the swarm can be huge, containing up to 120 million insects per square mile! In 1889, a swarm across the Red Sea covered 2,000 square miles (McComisky, 256). To prevent an outbreak of locusts in Cyprus in 1881, egg cases totaling a net weight of 1,300 tons were dug up by hand.

Not having experienced such a phenomenon, we can only faintly sense the horror of having a swarming, hopping, sun-darkening, chewing mass descend on your land. In 1915, journalist John D. Whiting stood almost where Joel stood in Jerusalem and recorded the following words: "Sudden darkening of the bright sunshine . . . clouds . . . so dense as to appear quite black . . . in an inconceivably short time every leaf is consumed, leaving bare and barked twigs only. . . . It seemed as if the entire surface of the ground moved, producing a most curious effect upon one's vision and causing dizziness. . . . Up and up the city walls and the castle they climbed to their very heights" (Brodsky, 34). The horror of the actual locust invasion would be repeated by its sober after effects. For agricultural people, locusts were disaster. Crops and animal feed were destroyed. Those lacking adequate stores or money to buy food could easily starve. Is it any wonder Joel was concerned?

The Day(s) of the Lord

Not only is the "day of the Lord" the dominant theme in Joel, but it occurs in six other Old Testament prophetic books as well—Isaiah (13:6, 9), Ezekiel (13:5; 30:3), Amos (5:18, 20), Obadiah (15), Zephaniah (1:7, 14) and Malachi (4:5). The idea of the day of the Lord is crucial to the Old Testament prophets. The New Testament also takes up the terminology. Passages such as 1 Corinthians 5:5, 1 Thessalonians 5:2, and 2 Peter 3:10 actually use the exact terminology of the prophets, "the day of the Lord," while others such as Matthew 11:22-24 and 1 Corinthians 1:8 transform the phrase to the "day of judgment," "the day of our Lord Jesus Christ," or "day of the Lord Jesus" (2 Cor. 1:14). All of this shows how crucial the concept is in the Bible.

It becomes clear immediately that the Bible and even Joel have in mind more than one "day of the Lord." This was suggested in the outline of Joel's book (see page 86). In Joel, three of the five occurrences of the phrase come in the first major section of the book, dealing with the locust plague (1:15; 2:1, 11). The last two uses come in Joel 2:31 and 3:14, which are part of the second section of the book.

If the "day of the Lord" is not a single event for Joel, what does it mean? For the Old Testament prophets, the day of the Lord is the time when God clearly comes near to visit the world and intervene in human history. Obviously, this can happen more than once. It can take place in connection with a locust plague, as in the first part of Joel. It will also happen, Joel predicts, in connection with the coming of the Spirit on all flesh (2:28-31). The second coming of Jesus, as predicted in the New Testament, is the greatest divine visitation and intervention of all time.

"The day of the Lord" terminology, then, is not so much about time or a specific single event as it is about a great theological concept. The concept is that God can and does work in human history to judge and to save.

In Joel there seem to be four major elements that are connected with this "day of the Lord":

1. *"Signs" precede, or are the initial part of, the day.* The famine and destruction brought by the locusts are a sign the day of the Lord is here (1:15-18). Darkness of sun, moon, and sky are related to the coming of the day. It is not clear in some places whether these signs immediately precede the day of the Lord or are actually a part of it (see 2:1, 2, 10, 11). In other verses (2:31, 32; 3:15), it is clear they occur before the actual day. God wants to inform and warn before the day arrives.

2. *Opportunity to repent or reach out to God is given in connection with "the day."* This opportunity could be a holy day of fasting and prayer (1:14), an appeal to repent and rend hearts (2:12, 13), or the simple declaration that calling on the name of the Lord saves (vs. 32). The day of the Lord is clearly an occasion for a decision for or against God (3:14). Along with the giving of the signs mentioned above, this implies that God not only wants to warn people, He also wants them to prepare for the day so they can be saved.

3. *Judgment on evil is a part of the day.* Destruction is part of the day (1:15; 2:3, 11). All nations are gathered for judgment (3:1, 2, 12). When God comes near to visit, evil forces will be dealt with.

4. *God's people are restored and blessed.* In Joel, God saves and restores His people after the locust plague (2:19, 20). In the day when the nations are judged, God's true people are blessed and delivered (3:16-21). The day of the Lord is good only if you are on God's side. Then you need not fear His visit.

Although one cannot point to a specific reference to each of these four elements every time the term "day of the Lord" is used in Scripture, I believe they are assumed from Joel's time onward. When later writers used the term, they assumed these four elements were all part of the package. Certainly, all four do fit together as a whole picture.

The time element of the day of the Lord is frustrating for some people. The scientific mind, which wants precise dates and times, finds Joel's statements on time less than satisfying. Statements such as "near" (1:15, 3:14) and "close at hand" (2:1) leave something to be desired.

In chapter 1 it appears as if the locusts have already arrived (1:4, 6), yet the "day of the Lord" is, according to 1:15, only "near." On the other hand, 2:11 seems to equate the day of the Lord with the arrival of the army of locusts. The best answer I can give is that the locust plague is part of the day of the Lord, but not the whole of it. The "day of the Lord" is related to the locusts, but it is much more as well. Perhaps we could diagram it as such:

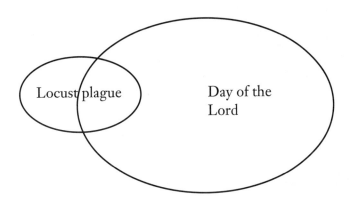

The larger restoration of Judah in the latter part of the book is a future event. According to Joel 2:28, it comes "afterward." The phrase "in those days and at that time" is clearly oriented to a different era than the time of the locusts.

Other than these references, it is difficult to pinpoint time using the book of Joel. We can begin to do so only as we look outside of Joel, which we will do shortly. Stay tuned.

In conclusion, we would do well to consider Joel as the crucial original source for much of what we have come to believe and appreciate in connection with the "day of the Lord" and the great final "day of our Lord Jesus Christ." So much of the basic outline, and even the details, of what other Old Testament writers and the New Testament teach is found here. The day is near, yet there is a lack of precise dates. The four elements that are closely related to the day and even the signs manifested in the sun, moon, and stars (Matt. 24:29; Rev. 6:12) are all present in our vision of the day of our Lord Jesus. All these concepts are rooted firmly in Joel's prophecy of so long ago.

Joel and Acts 2

By far, the most famous passage in Joel is 2:28-32 (in the Hebrew Bible it is 3:1-5). No less than nine different New Testament passages refer to this section of Joel: Matthew 24:29; Mark 13:24, 25; Luke 21:25; Acts 2:17-21, 39, 21:9, 22:16; Romans 10:13; Titus 3:6; and Revelation 6:12. The first recorded Christian sermon given by Peter on the day of Pentecost, uses this passage as its key text. Certainly this section deserves our careful attention.

The first part of this passage deals with the coming of the Spirit (2:28, 29). Three major points are emphasized:

1. The abundance of the Spirit. The Spirit is not given in small measure but "poured out." This word image portrays an abundant *flow* like a mighty rushing stream or flood. This flood of the Spirit causes people to prophesy, dream, and see visions. These actions are powerful, divine revelatory acts and testify to the overflowing gift of God's Spirit.

2. The universality of the Spirit. The revolutionary nature of the idea that the Spirit is poured out on *all* people cannot be emphasized enough. In Israel, the Spirit was generally reserved for mature, free men. Joel's promise of the Spirit in connection with the day of the Lord breaks that mold. The Spirit comes regardless of gender (male and female), age (old and young), or social status ("even on my *servants*," vs. 29). Basically, anyone can receive the divine gift of the Spirit.

Probably for Joel "all people" still meant all *Judahite* people. The passage talks of "your" sons and daughters, "your" old and young men (2:28). Only at a later time does the full revelation of what "all people" really means become known.

3. Intimate communion with God. The results of this abundant, universal outpouring are prophecy, dreams, and visions. These manifestations are all means of divine revelation to humankind. What God is doing through the Spirit is revealing Himself and coming into close communion with His people. When you receive communication from God, you are in intimate contact with Him.

The second part of this passage (vss. 20, 31) deals with the wonders and the cosmic signs that accompany the day of the Lord. God will do supernatural things. When Yahweh acts on His day, even the things that people take for granted as regular and immovable will be affected. Sun and moon are altered.

Earlier occurrences of God's special visitation had similar manifestations. The Exodus is an example. Wonders occurred (Exod. 4:21; 7:3, 9)—blood (Exod. 7:17-21), fire and smoke (Exod. 19:18), and darkness (Exod. 19:18). Some of these same things were also present in the locust plague of Joel. Darkness with sun and moon affected (2:2, 10) and fire (vss. 3, 4) are mentioned. God is warning His people about the great and dreadful day of the Lord (vs. 31; see also vs. 11).

The third and final part of the section (vs. 32) deals with the fate of people. Is there any hope on that "great and dreadful day"? The answer is a resounding Yes. God promises salvation and deliverance to all who call on His name. Again, the setting is local. Mount Zion and Jerusalem are specifically mentioned; it remains for a later time for God's universal salvation to be fully understood by His people and prophets.

When Peter quotes this passage on the day of Pentecost in Acts 2:17-21, he actually stays very close to what Joel says. He must have learned his memory verses well! The few differences that exist are, however, very instructive. Some have said these small variations come from Peter's use of a different translation of Joel. That is possible, and the most likely translation for Peter to use would be the Septuagint, the Greek version of the Old Testament. However, the variations do not seem to reflect the Septuagint.

I believe the difference is simply Peter's attempt, under the guidance of the Spirit, to make this text clearly relevant to his audience and time. It is interesting to notice how he does this as we look at the four adjustments he makes.

1. The simple "afterward" of Joel 2:28 becomes "in the last days God says" of Acts 2:17. Joel is preaching about a future event, and his time sequence is inherent in his book. A general reference to the future is appropriate. In Acts 2, Peter is talking about what he sees as a current fulfillment of Joel's prophecy. Peter has come to believe that Jesus' coming has brought on the last days or the end of the age. The way he phrases this message places it squarely in line with that belief.

2. At the end of Acts 2:18 Peter adds the phrase, "and they will prophesy." Joel's passage could easily be interpreted to *imply* this phrase because of the rules of Hebrew parallelism. In other words, what Joel implies, Peter states. Peter has good reason to emphasize prophecy by doing this. On the day of Pentecost, people have just seen the amazing result of the Spirit's outpouring. The disciples are not upper-class Jews, and Peter wants to make clear to people that prophecy by "servants" is what is expected in the last days.

3. While Joel says in 2:30 that God "will show wonders in the heavens and on the earth," Peter says in Acts 2:19; that God will "show wonders in the heaven above and *signs* on the earth below" (emphasis supplied). Peter wants to emphasize the presence of signs on earth as a signal of the day of the Lord. While the falling of the Spirit may be a part of those signs and wonders, the main thing Peter wants to point to is the ministry of Jesus as an evidence of the fulfillment of this passage. His very first statement explaining this passage portrays Jesus as a worker of miracles, signs, and wonders (Acts 2:22). For this reason, Peter highlights this part of the signs of Jesus' coming.

4. In Acts, Peter leaves off the last part of Joel 2:32, which localizes the salvation in the day of the Lord to Mount Zion and Jerusalem. Joel was clearly speaking to an audience of Judahites who were concerned about their city and temple. Peter is speaking to an audience of both local *and* international Jews from all over the middle eastern world. Both Joel's audience and Peter's hearers needed to know that the message applied to them. For Joel, that was best done by specific mention of local geography, while for Peter the leaving off of the local reference best fitted truth and his present hearers.

Peter has in no way violated the basic principles and thrust of Joel's message. What he has done is to adapt and apply those principles, under the Spirit's guidance to a new time and situation. Good preachers today do much the same thing. They take the eternal truth of the Word and apply it to their hearers. We can do the same thing.

Reasons, Judgment, and Salvation

One nice thing about Joel is his clear portrayal of what causes people to be on one side or the other in the decisive day of the Lord. While judgment comes to some—in particular, the nations—and salvation to others, we are not kept guessing as to how we end up on one side or the other. Let's begin with the bad news and then move on to the good news.

The basic concern of Joel 3 is the judgment of the nations. This happens when God sets out to restore the fortunes of Judah. Punishment of the nations is part of the restoration of Israel. If God's people are to be safe, their enemies must be taken care of.

Joel pictures a great gathering of the nations that will take place in the valley of Jehoshaphat (3:2, 12). Jehoshaphat means *Yahweh is Judge* and seems to be symbolic of a valley near Jerusalem. The name also could be alluding to God's great victory for Israel during the time of King Jehoshaphat (2 Chron. 20).

Joel specifically talks about gathering *all* nations (3:2, 12). Five nations/cities are specifically mentioned—Tyre, Sidon, Philistia (vs. 4), Egypt and Edom (vs. 19). Tyre and Sidon were twin cities northwest of Israel in Phonecia, while Philistia was southwest of Judah.

Edom is east of Israel, while Egypt is, of course, south. These specific names seem to illustrate that enemies all around Israel will be taken care of. Egypt and Edom are ancient enemies. God seems to be saying, "I'll deliver you from your enemies from *all* areas and *all* times."

These nations are not arbitrarily punished. God gives specific reasons for His judgments on them:

1. These nations have deported Israelites. The word Joel uses is *scattered* (vs. 2). The Assyrians and Babylonians clearly did this, and other deportations may also have occurred.

2. The nations have appropriated Israel's land. Yahweh terms this territory taken as *"my* land" (vs. 2). The taking of Israel's land is viewed as an affront to God Himself. Since God owns the land, the nations have stolen from the Almighty and must face the consequences.

3. The nations have sold the Israelites as slaves (vss. 3, 6, 7). It seems to particularly upset Joel that Jewish young people and children have been part of the slave trade of the nations (vss. 3, 8). The fact that the proceeds from the sale of these slaves were used for the sinful pleasures of immorality ("prostitutes" vs. 3) and wine makes it even worse. The money was not used for necessities but was wasted on idle pleasures.

4. The nations have plundered Israel's wealth. The gold, silver, and treasures of Israel have been carried off. Notice the repetition of the word *my* before each of these items (vs. 5). The wealth of Israel is Yahweh's. He has been robbed. Some scholars have suggested that this verse specifically refers to the plunder of the temple. This interpretation is possible, but since God owns everything in Israel, it is probably a more general statement about Israel's material goods, rather than simply referring to temple treasures.

It is interesting that no *religious* sins are mentioned. The nations are not condemned for their idolatry or polytheism. Neither are personal moral ethics referred to. The nations are not called liars or adulterers. Joel assumes that the nations may not know about God.

Personal ethics are related to religion and the covenant, so if God is not known, personal ethics are not at issue. These peoples are not even specifically condemned for invading Israel or going to war with them. As we read the prophets, we find that God, at times, uses foreign nations as His tools to discipline Israel (see, for example, Isa. 8:4-8). It would not be fair to fault the nations for any of these reasons, and thus God and Joel do not.

What God is concerned about is inhumanity to humanity. These nations have gone too far. They have treated Israel cruelly in the four ways listed earlier. They have done to others what they do not want for themselves. They have done things they *know* are not right. This is not acceptable to God. Known sins against people is what brings the judgment of God. People reap what they have done to others. This is Joel's theology, and I believe it should be taken seriously today as we look at nations around us. Certainly, it is against this background that we can understand Matthew 25:31-46. In this judgment scene which takes place in the Father's presence, people are cursed or blessed on the basis of how they treat others. Have those who use brutality in Rwanda, the former Yugoslavia, Chechnya, Turkey, and myriads of other places, heard this message? Have we realized the seriousness of our own cruelty? We would do well to listen.

Now the good news, or rather the path to good news. What should we do as we face the day of the Lord? How does one respond to God so that he or she may be part of the blessing God promises? What are the results of following the right path?

The first section of Joel (1:1–2:17) comes in an interesting package. In the face of this locust plague/day of the Lord, the people are summoned to weep/wail (1:5, 13), mourn (vss. 8, 9), and despair (vs. 11). Some have called the form of this section a national, or communal, lament. People are summoned to respond collectively as if attending a funeral. Israel seems to have a tradition of holding special services to deal with national tragedy. Judges 20:26 describes such a service prompted by a military defeat. Many believe Jeremiah 14 alludes to such a service at a time of severe drought. At such services people wept, mourned, wailed, prayed, and repented. Joel seems to be writing a liturgy or order of service for such a service of lamentation at the temple in Jerusalem.

At this religious service, not only the various segments of ordinary people such as elders (1:2), children (vs. 3), drunkards (vs. 5), and farmers (vs. 11) are to mourn, but so are the priests (1:9, 13; 2:17). God's house has been affected, as has the land in general. The priests are to lead in this service. They must declare the holy fast and call a sacred assembly at Jerusalem (2:15) to which all must attend (vs. 16). The priests are to plead for the people and ask God to spare them (vs. 17).

This national day of mourning is the setting for Joel's call to return to God with all the heart (vs. 12). Fasting, weeping and mourning are to accompany this return to God because they are clearly an essential part of such a day of lament. The lament called for is not to be just an outward kind of grief that shows itself only by tearing the garments in a typical cultural show of sorrow. The heart—the whole inner being—must be torn (vs. 13). People must feel and respond to the situation both internally and externally. They should return to God because they can trust His graciousness and compassion.

The truly good news is that when all this happens, God replies (vs. 19). God hears and responds with grace and compassion. In a sense, all that was done in connection with the national day of mourning is a part of "calling on the name of the Lord" (see especially 2:32). All who do this are saved. Since the process has already been described, Joel can later refer to the process in shorthand form. The clear message of Joel is one of hope. Those who go through this process of repentance, which includes the acts of this national day of mourning, will find that God is merciful enough and powerful enough to deliver.

This is a message for us today. I am afraid God's people today have forgotten about such things. Has your church in time of crisis ever been moved to respond with a special day of sorrow, mourning, prayer, and repentance—all the things Joel sees as part of "calling on the name of the Lord"? Perhaps Joel's book can serve as a model to us. If we want our church renewed, we can learn from this ancient prophet who knew what sorrow was and who was able to call his people to express it in a moving and tangible way.

■ Applying the Word

Joel 1–3

1. What crisis periods have I faced in my life when the horror and devastation seemed like a plague of locusts? In what terms could I describe such an experience that might help other people sense what I went through? Did this experience lead to a sense of God's presence, or did it lead to a sense of His absence? Why?

2. The day of the Lord always comes with signs. Do I see any signs around me that suggest God is about to visit the world in judgment and/or salvation? Should I look at the situation around me for "signs" of God's work? If so, how might that help me in my daily life? What are the dangers involved in looking for such signs?

3. Joel's time frame for the future is quite nebulous. How do I feel about God's timing in my life? Does God usually work in a somewhat flexible time frame, or does He have an exact schedule? What are the reasons for my answer? Is it better for me to know exactly when things will happen or to be somewhat unsure? Why?

4. Do I believe that the promise of the Spirit found in Joel and fulfilled in Acts has come true for me? Why? What is the evidence in my life? How would I know if the Spirit had been poured out on me? What do prophecy and dreams and visions mean for me today? Should these things be happening in my church? How? Why?

5. Should my church—local, regional, or worldwide—have days or times of national mourning, fasting, and praying as Joel did? What reasons can I give for my answer? If such times were held, what should be the reason for the

occasion? What should take place, and how should these occasions be conducted? What might be the results in the church?

■ Researching the Word

1. Joel twice mentions the darkening of the sun and moon (as well as the moon turning to blood) and the falling of the stars as signs of the "day of the Lord" (2:10, 31). These signs are used over and over in both Old and New Testaments. Using a concordance, look for other places in the Bible where these signs are mentioned. What does this teach you about the day of the Lord and the signs of its coming?
2. Joel 2:23, 24 speaks of the autumn and spring rains that fall in Israel. Using a Bible dictionary, look up the words "rain" and/or "farming" and "seasons." Try to understand the agricultural year in Israel. How does the understanding of farming, seasons, and rain relate to the spiritual life? Why does Joel mention that God gives both autumn and spring rains? Why are they mentioned in that order?
3. Romans 10:13 quotes Joel 2:32. Read the Romans passage carefully. On the basis of your reading and what you can learn from a Bible commentary, do you think Paul is using Joel 2:32 in the same way as Joel himself did? Does Paul use Joel 2:32 in the same way as Peter did in Acts 2:21? Give reasons for your answers.

■ Further Study of the Word

1. For general insights on locusts, see H. Brodsky, " 'An Enormous Horde Arranged for Battle,' Locusts in the Book of Joel."
2. For a good, concise description of the meaning of the "day of the Lord," see S. Horn, ed., *The SDA Bible Dictionary*, on "Day of the Lord." For more details, see a multi-volume Bible dictionary or encyclopedia on the same phrase.

PART THREE

Amos

Judgment on Injustice,
Perversion, and Pride

CHAPTER SEVEN

Introduction to Amos

Hosea tugs at our heartstrings. Joel makes us think about judgment and the day of the Lord. Amos confronts us with our behavior toward others and the nature of society. More clearly than any of the other prophets we will study, Amos causes us to ask questions about justice. How just and fair are we as we deal with other people?

Amos should make us think about our house, our cars, and how we get our money. He wants us to think about how we spend our money, and he wants us to see how others around us live. The affluent society of Amos's day, as well as the destitute classes that accompanied it, has many parallels for our time. What does it mean to live as fair, compassionate people today?

■ Getting Into the Word

To get an overview of Amos, read the book through, preferably in one setting. As you read, answer the following questions:

1. What are the specific sins Amos condemns in the nations of Judah and Israel? Do they differ from each other? How? Why?
2. Amos was an itinerant farmer. List the things in his book that show he was itinerant and visited various areas. Write down the things that suggest he was a farmer.

The Man

Like most of the Old Testament prophets, Amos gives us little information about himself. But we do have more information concerning him than we do for the first two prophets we have studied—Hosea and Joel. We are told what town he was from, what his occupation was, and when he prophesied.

Amos came from Tekoa, which was a Judahite village located about ten miles south of Jerusalem and six miles south of Bethlehem (Amos 1:1). We can better understand Amos's preaching about the northern kingdom if we remember that the border of the northern kingdom and the sanctuary at Bethel were only about fifteen miles from Amos's farm home in Tekoa. Samaria, the northern capital, was only a day's journey away using the transportation methods of that day.

Amos's profession, according to Amos 1:1, was a shepherd. This title can refer to a keeper of sheep and/or goats. In a later passage, 7:14, Amos calls himself one who "took care of sycamore-fig trees." Probably a more accurate translation would be one who "slits" or "pinches" figs (Stuart, 377). The sycamore fig tree was a large tree, but the figs were generally of an inferior type. Their quality was greatly enhanced if each fig was pinched or slit on the upper part of the fruit before it matured. The resulting fruit became sweeter and softer.

The climate of Tekoa was not conducive to sycamore figs, so Amos most likely performed this part of his work in another part of the region. His book does not tell us whether he owned his own flocks and fig orchards or whether he labored as a hired hand for others. Whatever the case, he was itinerant. Both his shepherding and fig-slitting took him to different places. Undoubtedly, the observations he made as he traveled informed and fueled his comments on Israel's situation before God.

The Historical Setting

The first verse of Amos places the book during the reign of Jeroboam (II), king of the northern kingdom of Israel, and that of Uzziah, ruler in the Judahite southern kingdom. Jeroboam II reigned from 786 to 746 B.C. Uzziah lived until 742 B.C. but took his son

Jotham into co-regency with him in 750 B.C. The fact that no other kings are mentioned suggests that Amos was not active as a prophet beyond 742 B.C. We have no idea how many years earlier he began his ministry.

Jeroboam was the final king of the northern kingdom's longest lasting dynasty. He was in the line of Jehu, which commenced in 842 B.C. In the 760s and 750s Israel reached its highest point in economic prosperity. Jeroboam restored the boundaries of the kingdom to the position they had enjoyed under Solomon—the first and only occasion that this occurred during post-Solomonic times (2 Kings 14:23-29). Several facts led to this wealth and expansion under Jerboam II.

Israel's three major enemies, Egypt, Babylon, and Assyria, were not very active during this period. Furthermore, in 805 B.C., Assyria had subdued Syria and thus destroyed the power that would have set limits on Jeroboam. Israel stepped into this power vacuum and gained control of extremely lucrative international trade routes.

This power and economic prosperity is the background for Amos's prophetic ministry. Political and economic progress had led to ethical and religious decline. Affluence, exploitation, and the profit motive were the most notable features of Israelite society (Motyer, *Day of the Lion*, 15). The rich had multiple houses (3:15) and could furnish them extravagantly while affording themselves every bodily indulgence (3:12; 4:1; 6:4, 6). On the other hand, the poor were destitute, oppressed, and exploited by an unjust and corrupt society and legal system (2:6, 7; 5:10, 12; 8:5). The book of Amos portrays a situation in which ostentatious wealth and consumption existed side by side with desperate poverty.

Religious worship centers were utilized by the people, and sacrifices were made, but religion was of the formal outward variety. Amos says God hates and despises all these religious forms because they are not accompanied by justice and righteousness (Amos 5:21-24).

The itinerant farmer Amos noticed all of these things. He was a student of his times and sensitized by the Spirit of God; he wrote God's message, which included God's commentary on the situation and an appeal to his generation.

Theme and Message

While Hosea emphasizes God's love, Amos stresses God's justice. Hosea reveals God's heart in its response to spiritual adultery, while Amos uncovers God's feelings in the face of unfairness and abuse of others. God will not stand idly by while Israel practices the outward form of religion but destroys people. In spite of the fact that things seem good now, judgment is coming. The future is not bright, but is filled with darkness because of Israel's sin. The essence of the book is probably best captured in 5:18-24, which is God's response to empty religious formality and His call for justice.

The God of Amos, however, is not simply the God of Israel and Judah. He also rules the destinies of Syria, Tyre, Edom, Ammon, and Moab (1:3–2:3). Yahweh is Lord of all nations. These neighbors of Israel face judgment, and God is specific in His reasons for action against them. These nations have also been unjust in their actions.

Amos has long been a favorite book of defenders of social justice and critics of formal state religions. A friend tells me it was one of the few religious books that Communists in the former Soviet Union were encouraged to read and study. The God of the Old Testament has always been a defender of the poor and needy, and Amos's book is a prime example of that attitude. We can certainly use its message today.

Outline of Amos
Judgment on Injustice, Perversion, and Pride

I. Prophecies against the nations and Israel (1:1–5:17)
   A. Title and Introduction (1:1, 2)
   B. Prophecies against Israel's neighbors (1:3–2:3)
   C. Prophecy against Judah (2:4, 5)
   D. Prophecy against Israel (2:6–5:17)
II. Exile, Divine Retribution, and Restoration (5:18–9:15)
   A. Judgment on the religious, the complacent, the proud (5:18–6:14)
   B. Parables and symbols of judgment (7:1–9:10)
   C. Israel's restoration (9:11-15)

CHAPTER EIGHT

Prophecies Against the Nations and Israel

Amos 1:1–5:17

Amos proves himself to be a clever communicator in the first section of his book. A prophet, who must convey a message of judgment to his people, is faced with a challenge. How do you get people to listen to a message about themselves that they don't want to hear or might even get angry about?

Amos's tactic is to begin by preaching about something his audience will want to hear—something they long to see happen. For Israel, that is a message about Yahweh's judgment on Israel's foreign neighbors. If you listen, you can almost hear the cheers that come when the farmer from Tekoa begins to proclaim the disaster about to befall the surrounding nations. Most of his hearers are probably still rejoicing when he gets to their brother Judah to the south. How right and fitting that their God defends His people by actions against their enemies!

Following loud and hearty amens, Amos suddenly switches gears. God is about to judge Israel itself. Israelites can't escape just because they claim to be God's people. They have sinned, and a God who is just must respond. God's judgment on Israel proves to be much broader and more extensive than on any other nation. Amos is not hesitant to spell it out in detail, and we will look carefully at it as we explore this first section of Amos.

■ Getting Into the Word

Amos 1:1–2:6

Read Amos 1:1–2:6 through twice. As you read, answer the following questions:

1. Amos 1:2 summarizes, in one verse, the thrust of Amos's message. Look at the verse carefully. When it says the Lord "roars" and "thunders," what is Yahweh being likened to? Compare this imagery with Jeremiah 25:30 and Joel 3:16. Why is this symbolism used? Where is God "roaring" from? What is the significance of these two places? What is the result of God's roaring? Using a Bible dictionary and/or atlas, find out the meaning of "Carmel." After doing this, write out your thoughts on the overall meaning of this verse.

2. Make a list of the non-Jewish nations or cities that Amos condemns in chapters 1 and 2. Locate them on a map, and find out a bit about them by consulting a good Bible dictionary. Why is this particular group of places mentioned? Is there any reason for the order in which they appear?

3. In many of the judgments, chapters 1 and 2 mention kings or rulers—sometimes by name. What is said about these kings and rulers? Why do you think they are mentioned specifically?

4. Amos 2:4, 5 condemns the southern kingdom of Judah. List Judah's sins as given in these chapters. How are they different from the sins of the surrounding nations? Why are different sins mentioned? What does this tell us about how God judges?

■ Exploring the Word

Yahweh, the Lion King

After introducing Amos and his times in Amos 1:1, the book launches immediately into its message. In one short, terse verse (vs. 2), the basic thrust of the book is summarized. Unpacking the meaning of this verse helps us sense the essence of the book.

Amos's message begins with "the Lord," or Yahweh, the covenant God of Israel. This is not just any generic God who is speaking. Israel must realize that the God who revealed Himself and His special Name to His people Israel at the time of the Exodus (Exod. 6:1-8) is the one who is speaking to them.

This God, this Yahweh, "roars" and "thunders" (vs. 2). The significance of this terminology lies in its direct comparison of God to a *lion*. One British author titled his book on Amos, *The Day of the Lion* (Motyer). Joel (3:16) and Jeremiah (25:30) use similar terminology, but Amos emphasizes the picture more. Not only does he make the comparison in this all-important theme verse, but he refers to this same idea when he declares in Amos 3:8, "The lion has roared—who will not fear? The Sovereign Lord has spoken—who can but prophesy?"

Reading these passages makes it clear that the roaring lion of Amos is *not* a defanged, declawed, purring house cat. The lion of Amos is a powerful, fearsome lion that is bent on judgment. He roars from his den in Jerusalem, the Holy City and site of the temple. Even though Amos speaks his message to the northern kingdom of Israel, the clear message is that the Jerusalem temple, in the southern kingdom, is still God's dwelling place—the home of the lion.

When the lion king Yahweh roars, drought comes. The "pastures of the Shepherd" which dry up are probably the lowland grazing areas of the south that Amos is familiar with. The top of Carmel is the summit of Mount Carmel in the north. Yahweh's judgment brings dryness from the low pastures to the mountain heights, from the south to the north. The drought judgment is pictured as universal.

The form of this verse is that of a covenant curse announcement. Amos is proclaiming that Yahweh is about to act and put into effect the curses promised in the covenant. Such announcements are usually couched in this way. One covenant curse promises harm from wild animals as a judgment for covenant breaking (Lev. 26:22; Deut. 32:24). Yahweh, the Lion, carried out that curse.

Drought also fulfills a curse promise (Lev. 26:19; Deut. 28:22-24). Dryness of the shepherd's pastures and of the peak of Mount Carmel fulfill that curse. Drought could, of course, bring on other agricultural disasters and the general desolation of the land. The roar of the Lion has broad-reaching effects.

Amos 3:8 clearly makes judgment the primary message of Amos. Yahweh's covenant with Israel has been violated, and the covenant curses spelled out in detail in the Pentateuch (Deut. 28:15-68) are about to fall. Israel must quake at the Lion's roar.

Yahweh, the Lion, is a problem for many believers today. We prefer Yahweh, the compassionate Parent and solicitous Shepherd. We can deal with a loving, merciful God, but the Lion who roars and enacts curses troubles us. We live in an age when many desire to domesticate God. We want to turn the Lion of Amos into a purring pet. We must remember that it is sin on the part of Israel and the righteousness and holiness of a covenant-keeping God that creates the lion. Sin today is just as dangerous and just as capable of creating the Lion. Amos will have performed a great service if he helps us remember that.

God Judges the Neighbors

After introducing his judgment message in 1:2, Amos immediately launches into a series of judgment messages against the nations. As mentioned in the Introduction, this is a wonderful communication technique which leads his listeners/readers to agree with him before they hear/read of the judgment they themselves will receive.

Each of these judgment messages are introduced by a set formula— "For three sins of . . . , even for four, I will not turn back my wrath" (1:3, 6, 9, 11, 13; 2:1, 4). This formula emphasizes the multiplicity of sins. God does not move in judgment on one or two sins. The countries needing judgment in this case have sinned many times. They constitute repeat offenders.

The nations and cities chosen for condemnation are not a haphazard group. They are all close neighbors of Israel. The first three mentioned lie north and west of Israel and are traditional enemies. Damascus (1:3) is a major city north of Israel and stands for the country of Syria. Gaza (vs. 6) lies in Philistia, which is west of Israel, and represents that nation as do its sister cities—Ashdod (vs. 8) and Ashkelon (vs. 8). The city-nation of Tyre (vs. 9) is northwest of Israel.

The next three nations lie east and south of Israel, and all have some relationship to Israel. Edom (vs. 11) traces its heritage to Esau, Jacob's older brother. Ammon (vs. 13) and Moab (2:1) were founded by sons of Lot, Abraham's nephew (Gen. 19:36-38).

The progression in Amos seems to move from traditional enemies of Israel who are nearby to neighbors who have blood relationships to Israel. In this light we should remember that following Moab, the next nation to be condemned is Judah (2:4, 5), which is Israel's full brother to the south. Thus the judgment comes closer and closer to home as Amos proceeds down the list. Bit by bit, the prophet is zeroing in.

Amos seems to be especially disturbed by the kings of these nations. The line of Hazael, king of Damascus (842-766 B.C.) is mentioned (vs. 4). So are the kings of Beth Aven and Beth Eden (vs. 5).

In similar terminology, the rulers of Ashdod and Ashkelon are condemned (vs. 8) as are the kings of Ammon and Moab, along with their officials (1:15; 2:3). Destruction comes to the royal house in each case, with the exception of Ammon, where the king is said to go into exile.

Why is royalty singled out for judgment? The specific answer is not given in the text, but context and history suggest at least two reasons. In a day when kings had absolute power, they bore special responsibility for the sins of the nation. The prophets always portray leaders—political as well as religious—as particularly at fault when things go awry.

In particular, Amos condemns the rich and upper classes for their sins against the poor and oppressed. The king and his officials are the ultimate example of the rich, upper class. As such, they need judgment more than others. For Syria, royalty is destroyed, while common people merely go into exile (1:5).

God's condemnation of Israel's six non-Jewish neighbors follows a pattern already begun in the book of Joel. These neighbors do not know Yahweh and have not entered into any covenant with Him. The covenant blessings do *not* apply in their case—nor do the curses. They have no Pentateuch, Torah, or Ten Commandments. Then on what basis are they judged? What are the sins for which God condemns them?

Damascus (Syria) has treated her neighbor Gilead with extreme cruelty, threshing her like grain (1:3). At that time, grain was usually threshed by animals pulling a heavy wooden sled studded with wood or metal spikes across the grain. The vivid picture of driving such a sled with iron spikes over people conveys a powerful image of inhumanity (vs. 3). This forms the basis for God's judgement of Damascus.

Philistia (Gaza) has taken "whole communities" captive, selling them into slavery in Edom (vs. 6). To take slaves for yourself when you need them to work is one thing. To take them to resell for money is worse.

Edom has not only participated with Philistia in the slave trade; he has also stifled all compassion and pursued his brother (someone close he should have cared for) with the sword (vs. 11). Most Bible students believe "brother" in this case refers to Israel (Obad. 8-10).

Ammon has ripped open pregnant women merely to extend the borders of the country (1:13), while Moab has burned the bones of Edom's king (2:1). This latter event was done out of spite simply to add insult to injury.

All of these deeds are cruel acts of vengeance against people. These events constitute what we would today call war crimes and atrocities. The Bible does not directly condemn war itself, but it does condemn hateful, revengeful, and spiteful disregard of people and their feelings.

This passage contains a strong warning to all nations today—both those who make no claims of religious convictions and those who do. All nations are together in this one thing before God. No matter who you are, these kinds of activities will be judged. God will punish war crimes against people. Rwanda, Sudan, Bosnia, China (and others), are you listening?

This passage also makes it clear that Yahweh cares about and is involved in international affairs. All nations are under His observation and power, and He will intervene to judge cruel nations and save innocent peoples even when they do not acknowledge Him as Lord. We should not only teach these truths, but take comfort in them.

God Judges Judah

The message of judgment on Judah is different. She is condemned for two things. First, she has rejected God's law and failed to follow His decrees (vs. 4a). While disobedience is clearly implied here, much more is involved. Judah has not just failed to keep some particular statute, she has violated her covenant agreement with Yahweh. That covenant defined a personal relationship between Israel and her divine redeemer. Rejecting God's instruction is rejecting God.

Related to the first problem, and perhaps stemming from it, is the second condemnation. Israel has been led astray by false gods (vs. 4b). The people have foolishly returned to their ancestral deities (vs. 4b). Idolatry and spiritual adultery are implied. Judah clearly knows more than do the other nations and thus is responsible for more. God's reasons for judgment always fit the case. Judah is judged for her covenant breaking and idolatry because she should have known better!

With the judgment on Judah, Amos has declared seven judgments. Seven was an important number for Jews and often implied completeness. People in Amos's day knew how to count. Many thought that seven judgments would complete the judgment cycle. They rejoiced in the judgment which would fall on their neighbors, for they believed it meant they would be safer.

Many in Israel were not prepared for what was to happen next, although some may have sensed it. Judgment was about to be proclaimed on Israel, their own nation! The judgment can even be said to climax with Israel. The longest judgment pronounced so far in Amos takes up three verses; Israel is about to be condemned for almost eight chapters! Let us examine what God has to say to Israel, remembering that those who cheer the judgment of others will in the end be judged themselves!

■ Getting Into the Word

Amos 2:6–5:17

Read Amos 2:6–5:17 carefully twice. As you read, look for answers to the following questions:

1. **Amos 2:6-12 contains Amos's basic indictment of Israel for her sins. Read this passage carefully, and make a list of the sins of Israel. How do the sins of Israel compare to the sins of the**

surrounding nations and of Judah? Are they different? How?

2. Amos 4:4 says, "Go to Bethel" and "go to Gilgal," while Amos 5:5 says "Do not seek Bethel, do not go to Gilgal." How can you reconcile this seemingly contradictory counsel? These two places are mentioned over and over in this passage—Bethel in 3:14; 4:4; 5:5, 6; and Gilgal in 4:4; 5:5. Why are these places significant? You can find help in a Bible dictionary or commentary.

3. The first part of Amos 3 (vss. 1-8) gives a rationale and a basis for Amos's prophesying. People may have wondered why he was so bold to proclaim such a harsh message. This passage gives the reason. What is the meaning of the rhetorical questions in 3:3-6, 8? Summarize in your own words what Amos is saying 3:1-8.

4. Make a list of the consequences Israel faces because of her sins. What aspects of life will be affected?

■ Exploring the Word

Israel's Sin

As Amos has pronounced God's judgment on Israel's neighbors, the Israelites have cheered him on. Now the cheering stops. Using the same formula introduction that stands at the beginning of the first seven judgments, Amos now begins the proclamation of Israel's judgment. She who has been smug in her prosperity is also a habitual sinner, a repeat offender. The Lord's judgment falls on her as well as her neighbors. The details of the indictment come in Amos 2:6-12. Note them carefully.

1. "They sell the righteous for silver, and the needy for a pair of sandals" (*vs. 6b*). One of the main features of Hebrew poetry is parallelism of thought. This verse is an example of synonymous parallelism in which the two halves of the verse convey the same thought. The righteous and the needy are thus connected to each other. This verse presents a case in which those who have done no wrong, but who are simply poor and needy, are sold into slavery. In Bible times, slavery was often the result of debt. People who could not pay their bills were sold into slavery, often for a paltry sum, i.e., the price of a pair of sandals.

Slavery was not illegal in Bible times. The Bible lays down stipulations regarding it which try to make it more humane (Exod. 21:2-11, 20, 21, 26, 27; Deut. 15:12-18; 23:15, 16). What has happened here is a perversion of the system. Poor, needy people, who according to the covenant were to be helped, are turned into debt slaves by corrupt individuals—either by rigged court cases with unjustly high fines (Stuart, 317) or by unfair accounting methods.

2. *"They trample on the heads of the poor . . . and deny justice to the oppressed" (2:7a)*. This is a general statement referring to the same situation to which the specific example in verse 6b alludes. It is becoming clear that the rich are generally oppressing the poor and treating them cruelly. This certainly includes debt slavery (vs. 6b) and perversion of the justice system (vs. 7a—"deny justice"), as well as general mistreatment. These acts, particularly the denial of justice, are in direct violation of God's covenant commands (Exod. 23:6-8).

3. *"Father and son use the same girl" (2:7b)*. The identity of the girl is unclear; she may be a household servant. It is evident that father and son are explicitly forbidden to have sex with the same woman (Lev. 18:7, 8, 15; 20:11, 2; Deut. 27:20). Sexual morality is part of holiness, and to violate the laws regarding sexual behavior profanes Yahweh's holy name (Lev. 18:21). Although it is not clearly stated in the passage, implication is that the woman in this case is an unwilling participant; oppression may have put her in such a position that she could not refuse or had no recourse. Sexual immorality was rampant in Israel, and probably included what today we would call sexual abuse.

4. *"They lie down beside every altar on garments taken in pledge. In the house of their god they drink wine taken as fines" (2:8)*. What is shocking is that these oppressive slave-making, sexually reprobate people of Israel act religious! They visit the religious altars and shrines. Although they are not portrayed as worshiping Yahweh, they do have a form of religion. The strange thing is that in their very acts of

worship they break the covenant. Outer garments taken in pledge were to be returned by sunset because they were necessary to sleep warmly at night (Exod. 22:26, 27). Especially needy people, such as orphans and widows, were not to have their cloaks taken at all (Deut. 24:17, 18)! Wine taken in unjust fines is used for religious celebration!

5. *"You made the Nazirites drink and commanded the prophets not to prophesy" (2:12).* God's plan was to raise up prophets and Nazirites as religious leaders (vs. 11), but the Israelites have corrupted and silenced the very ones who might have helped them avoid their sin. Prophets and Nazirites, although different, are lumped together in this instance as examples of religious leadership. Nazirites made special vows to refrain from wine and anything having to do with grapes (Num. 6:1-21). They also shaved their heads and were to avoid the dead. Forcing them to drink wine made them break their vows and compromise their position. Commanding the prophets not to prophesy silenced their voices and severely hampered their ability to communicate since most people heard them orally rather than reading their written words. Amos evidently knew from personal experience what this was like, because he was forbidden to speak at Bethel (Amos 7:13).

In summary, Amos is saying to Israel: "You are deeply involved in social sins of cruelty and oppression. You have corrupted the legal system, and you are sexually immoral. Yet you think you are religious! You deceive yourselves and break the covenant even as you practice your religion. You destroy the effectiveness of the very prophets and Nazirites who could help you. You are in deep trouble!"

Over and over in his book, Amos plays on the same themes. It is as if he is hoping and praying that by saying these things repeatedly, light will dawn, and the people will catch on and repent.

Bethel and Gilgal

One particularly interesting aspect of Israel's sin is the issue of going to Bethel and Gilgal. In Amos 4:4, Amos says in a sarcastic tone, "Go to Bethel and *sin*; go to Gilgal and sin yet more" (emphasis supplied). Israel is determined to sin, so the people may as well go there and do so! On a more somber note, a serious appeal to seek Yahweh comes in Amos 5:5 that says, "Do *not* seek Bethel, do not go to Gilgal" (emphasis supplied). Clearly, sin is involved in going to these places. Why?

Bethel has a long history as a holy place going back even to before the Israelites were in Palestine. The name literally means "house of El." *El* was the Old Canaanite name for God. The town lies eighteen miles north of Jerusalem, and its role in Israel goes all the way back to the time of Noah (Gen. 28:17-22). The town remained an important religious center in the time of the judges (Judg. 20:28). When Solomon died and the kingdom was split into the northern kingdom of Israel and the southern kingdom of Judah, Jeroboam, the first Israelite king, made the place an official center of worship (1 Kings 12:28-32). At the time of Amos, Bethel was a royal sanctuary, the place where the king worshiped (Amos 7:13).

Gilgal was located between Jericho and the Jordan River. Israel camped there after crossing the Jordan (Josh. 3, 4), and Saul was crowned king of Israel in Gilgal. Gilgal is condemned by Amos and other prophets as a royal sanctuary with a corrupt sacrificial cult (Hos. 4:15; 9:15; 12:11; Amos 4:4; 5:5; Mic. 6:5).

The reason worship at these places is sin or rebellion is based on several considerations: (1) They are not the proper places for worship—Jerusalem is; (2) they are used for worship in a manner that is not fitting, i.e., people brag about their worship at these places (Amos 4:5); and (3) people have substituted such worship for righteous and just behavior (5:21-27).

This whole discussion tells us that religious worship and practice, in and of itself, can be abhorrent to God! False piety is sin. Piety practiced while engaging in injustice and immorality is not only worthless, it is rebellion! Israel is obviously in deep trouble.

Amos Explains

Amos 3:1-8 is the rationale Amos gives for his message and mission. Why is God speaking to Israel like this? Why does Amos dare open his mouth to preach? In a series of poignant images and vivid word pictures posed as questions, Amos answers these questions and objections. Amos makes clear in this passage the identity of Israel as God's chosen people and his role as a prophet called by the word of a sovereign Lord.

The first part of this section, verses 1 and 2, becomes very direct and personal about Yahweh and Israel. The pronouns show God addressing the people directly. "I" and "you" denote a close relationship. In this close relationship, God makes several things clear: (1) God's judgment, which He has expressed, is against *all* Israel—everybody who came out of Egypt (vs. 11). He doesn't single out only some of the people or merely one part of the kingdom. The whole people are involved. (2) Two things make these people special. First, God has delivered them from Egyptian slavery (vs. 1b). This salvation makes the people unique. Second, they are the only people God has chosen of all the different families of the earth (vs. 2). This idea refers back to God's original choice of Abraham in Genesis 12:1-3. These two statements sum up all that makes Israel God's special people. (3) Points one and two, rather than leading to exemption from judgment, form the basis for judgment. Therefore (see 3:2b), Amos says, because of your special privileges, you will be punished for your sins. Instead of responding with justice and righteousness to God's special treatment, Israel has responded with sin. In that situation, being a special people opens them to judgment in a unique way. Privilege leads to responsibility, not coddling. God's righteous judgment is the only responsible answer He can give to their sin.

Amos must now go on to answer the second question: What right does he have to say all these things? Amos responds to that unspoken question in chapter 3:3-8. Amos uses the number seven. He asks seven rhetorical questions and expects people to respond quickly with a spontaneous "No" answer. "Do two walk together unless they be agreed?" (vs. 3). No, of course not! Does a lion roar . . . when he has no prey?" (vs. 4). No, certainly not! At the end of the seven questions, Amos affirms that God will certainly reveal His plans to His servants the prophets (vs. 7). The voice of Yahweh is like the roar of the lion. One cannot help but pay attention.

In essence Amos is saying, "I did not choose this job! I can't help myself! God has spoken to me and given me a message, and the natural result is that I must prophesy." Amos does not have an identity crisis. He knows who he is—a spokesman for God—and he is not apologetic about it. One senses that after this explanation, no more is needed. Amos can continue with his ministry. People may not like what he says, but at least they know the reason for his actions.

Results of Sin

The last question to be answered deals with the results of sin. The nature of Israel's sins have been clearly spelled out. The basis of judgment and Amos's authority have been clarified. Israel deserves judgment. But what is going to happen?

God says bluntly that Israel will be punished for *all* her sins (vss. 2, 14). What does the punishment consist of? Israel will be crushed as though run over by a loaded cart (2:13). Even those who might think that they would escape will not. The swift, the strong, the warrior, the archer, the fleet-footed soldier, the horseman, and the bravest warriors will all be lost (2:14-16). They will not be able to save their own lives.

At least some of this will happen by military invasion (3:11). Israel's religious shrines will be plundered (vs. 14). The ornate houses of the rich will be demolished (vs. 15). Famine, drought, and plague will strike (4:6-10). Things will be so bad, in fact, that Amos sings a funeral lament over Israel (5:1ff).

Why does Amos point out all these horrible things? Why do I insist on listing them? I don't think Amos or the other prophets can really be understood unless we listen carefully to what is being said. We live in a time when people don't want to face the harsh realities of judgment and punishment. We would rather pass over these things lightly or explain them away. We are not so unique. I think Israel felt the same way. She would have liked to see Amos and his message disappear. We have already seen how Amos was forbidden to speak his message in Bethel. Nobody really enjoys this kind of sermon. You must force people to hear it, but hear it they must. Sinful, evil deeds bring inevitable consequences. If Yahweh is a moral, ethical God, He must operate ethically and morally. Just as children must learn that touching fire hurts and burns, so must humans learn that touching sin burns also. The message is not pleasant, but it is an important fact and crucial to understanding God and the world. If God didn't send the message to us, He would not be doing His job. If Amos failed to speak it or if I failed to make it clear, we would not be following our calling. "But," you may say, "is there any hope?" For the answer to that question, you must stay tuned.

■ Applying the Word

Amos 1:1–5:17

1. **Amos was affected, and his message was influenced, by the fact that he was an itinerant farmer. How have you been affected by your work or occupation? How do the things you see daily affect the way you speak to others about God and religion? Is this good or bad? Why?**

2. **Does Amos's condemnation of the rich apply today? Why? Are the poor oppressed by economic conditions today? How? What could well-off people do today to best help the poor? Who are the righteous poor today?**

3. **If God were to speak judgment through a prophet to your country today, what would He say? Would it be more like His condemnation of the surrounding nations or of Judah or of Israel? Why? Try writing a brief judgment on your country patterned after Amos's formula, "For three sins of _____, even for four."**

4. **Amos compares God to a roaring lion. Do you like that image of God? Why, or why not? If you were to compare God to an animal, which one do you think would fit best? What does your choice teach you about your own theology?**

5. **How might Amos's condemnation of a religious piety that lacks ethics and a concern for others apply today? Do you see any situation in which people act very pious and reli-**

gious but treat others in oppressive or unloving ways? Have you ever done so?

6. How do you react to Amos's clear portrayal that God punishes people for their sins? Why? Is this true, or is it just Amos's perception? Does God still punish for sins today? Give examples and reasons for your answer. What do you think should be God's response to sin?

■ Researching the Word

1. Using a concordance, look up the various references to the word *lion*. You can also learn more about the history of lions in Bible times by looking under "lion" in a good Bible dictionary. What kind of picture emerges? You might want to ask yourself why prophets such as Amos compare God to a lion, while Peter (1 Pet. 5:8) compares the *devil* to a roaring lion.

2. Read Judges 13:5 and Numbers 6:1-21, which deal with Nazirites and their vows. Using a Bible concordance, study passages and explanations dealing with Nazirites. Compare your findings with those of a Bible dictionary. Try to understand what it meant to be a Nazirite. What stands out in your mind as important? Do we have any group of people today comparable to Nazirites?

■ Further Study of the Word

1. For general insights, see Ellen G. White, *Prophets and Kings*, 279-292. Although this reference was suggested reading in an earlier chapter, it becomes more meaningful in the context of Amos.

2. For an interesting and provocative updating of Amos's prophecy to modern times, see Corbett, *Prophets on Main Street*, 15-30.

3. For more insight into what it was like to raise fruit and keep livestock in the time of Amos, see Thompson, *Handbook of Life in Bible Times*, 135-149.

CHAPTER NINE

Exile, Divine Retribution, and Restoration

Amos 5:18–9:15

The first part of Amos's book contained the opening salvos against Israel. In this second part, the prophet presses the attack. One can sense that Israel's fate needs to be clearly spelled out in more detail if the message is to get across. Amos proceeds to do just that.

This section of the book has three major parts. In the first part, 5:18–6:14, the prophet states clearly three times that Israel will go into exile and be oppressed (5:27, 6:7, 14). The nation will fall, and Amos specifically spells out three sins that will bring about this fall—religious formalism, complacency, and pride. The second major part, Amos 7:1–9:10, gives five symbolic visions that vividly portray the judgment that is about to take place.

The final section, Amos 9:11-15, talks of restoration. According to the prophet, there is some hope. That hope lies in the sovereign work of Yahweh, who will act on behalf of His people.

■ Getting Into the Word

Amos 5:18–9:15

Read Amos 5:18–9:15 thoughtfully twice. As you do so, work on answering the following questions:

1. Amos 5:18-20 speaks of "the day of the Lord." What does Amos teach about the day of the Lord? How does his teaching compare with what Joel taught on the same subject? How

does God's statement—that He hates and despises Israel's feasts—which immediately follows this passage relate to the day of the Lord?

2. Amos 6:1-7 condemns complacency. Make a list of the things Amos says about the Israelites' lifestyle. According to Amos, are these things wrong? What has Israel neglected to do?

3. Amos speaks of God "relenting" (7:3, 6). In some versions, this word is actually translated as "repent." Both translations give the clear implication that God is changing His mind. What do these verses actually mean? How do they relate to Malachi 3:6? Does God change? Why? What does this teach us about God?

4. The encounter between Amaziah and Amos is fascinating (see Amos 7:10-17). What does Amaziah tell Amos to do? Why? Few prophetic passages apply directly to one person other than the king, but here Amos does just that. What does he say about Amaziah? What do you think happened as a result of this encounter?

5. What is the meaning of the vision of the basket of ripe fruit (8:1-14)? Why would this vision have had special meaning for Amos? Several times in this vision the phrases "in that day" or "the days are coming" are used (8:3, 9, 11, 13). What do you think these phrases mean?

6. Based on Amos's restoration passage (9:11-15), list what God will do for Israel. Is any response from Israel called for? Why? Is the impression given that this restoration will cancel the judgment God has promised or that it will come after the judgment is completed? Why? What does this say about God?

■ Exploring the Word

Woe on Israel

Amos begins this part of his book with three messages of "woe." Two literally begin with the words "woe," while the final one begins with the words, "I abhor" (5:18; 6:1, 8).

Appropriately, this message of woe follows verses which speak of the wailing and anguish that accompany sorrow for the dead (5:16, 17). The natural setting of these passages is a funeral. The very use of the word *woe*, would take the hearers' minds back to the scene of mourning rites for the dead. The prophets took this form of funeral lament and used it for their proclamation of judgment. The very form of the words conveyed the solemnity and seriousness of their message. When these laments were heard, the most natural question would be, "Who died?" The answer, implied by Amos, is that "Your nation is in the process of dying!"

The first section (vss. 18-27) starts with a reference to the day of the Lord (vss. 18-20). That day, Amos says, will be a day of darkness, not light. In contrast to Israel's optimistic view of the day of the Lord as a time when the nation will be delivered from her enemies, Amos sees the day pessimistically. In the Old Testament, darkness means trouble, distress, misery, and even death (see 1 Sam. 2:9; Job 5:14; Ps. 35:6; Isa. 5:30; 49:9). Amos is clearly saying that Israel expects deliverance, but in reality faces destruction. Israel needs to revise her expectations drastically because she will be horribly disappointed. She may think she will find safety in the day of the Lord, but instead, she will meet danger.

The book of Joel, which we studied earlier, has a comprehensive view of the day of the Lord. Joel saw that day as a time of both judgment and restoration. Amos does not deal with the day of the Lord in as much depth. He seems satisfied to emphasize only the judgment side of the day's meaning and attempts to correct false views of the day, which seem only optimistic. In later passages of the book that refer to the same days of the Lord as "that day," Amos also deals exclusively with the judgment aspect of the "day" (8:3, 8, 11).

Immediately following Amos's words about the day of the Lord come the passages for which Amos is most famous:

> I hate, I despise your religious feasts;
> I cannot stand your assemblies.
> Even though you bring me burnt offerings and grain
>   offerings,

I will not accept them.
Though you bring choice fellowship offerings,
I will have no regard for them.
Away with the noise of your songs!
I will not listen to the music of your harps.
But let justice roll on like a river,
righteousness like a never-failing stream! (Amos 5:21-24).

Here Amos expresses God's deep feelings over the situation in Israel in which people do religious acts and sing pious songs but fail to act justly and righteously toward the oppressed in their society.

The next verse, "Did you bring me sacrifices and offerings forty years in the desert, O house of Israel?" (vs. 25) seems to imply that during the desert experience Israel had no system of offerings. According to Exodus and Leviticus, the sacrificial system was given in the wilderness, but it was especially designed for people in a settled situation with normal food production. Grain and wine offerings assume agricultural production. The system, therefore, seems to have gone into effect in a complete way only when Israel settled in Canaan.

The implied answer to the question in Amos 5:25, then, is "No." You did *not* bring me (full) sacrifices and offerings in the desert. The idea is that God and Israel had a good relationship in the wilderness, even without the full, regular observance of the sacrificial system. Systems may be helpful but are not necessary. Israel's concept that she could have favor with God by following the system is very mistaken! Instead, God demands justice and mercy. They matter the most.

In conclusion, then, how does Amos's discussion of the day of the Lord fit with his following passage on God's abhorrence of religious form without justice? In the messages of the prophets, the explanation of sin usually precedes the announcement of judgment. Sometimes, however, that order is reversed. Amos does just that and proclaims first the horror to come in a dark "day of the Lord." Then he makes clear in this passage the wrongdoing responsible for this judgment. The final result of Israel's sin is exile, and thus the cycle of announcement of judgment, declaration of sin, and end result is complete.

The next funeral song (6:1-7) condemns the sin of complacency and addresses those who feel secure on Mt. Samaria and in Zion. Although Amos's message is primarily against the northern kingdom, he doesn't forget that the southern kingdom is guilty of some of the same sins. He mentions Zion (Jerusalem) so that the southern kingdom doesn't get too cocky and the northern kingdom can't fault him for biased coverage.

This section contains a powerful play on the Hebrew word *rosh*, which means literally "head," "top," or "first." Amos 6:1 speaks of the "foremost nation," or "head nation," referring to the supposed position of Israel. In their new prosperity, God's people arrogantly see themselves as number one. This "head nation" also uses the "head" (NIV, "finest") lotions (vs. 6). In verse 7, at the conclusion of the section, God tells Israel that she will also be at the head of the line when it comes to punishment—"the first to go into exile." The same Hebrew word, *rosh*, is used in verses 1, 6, and 7. Those who complacently and arrogantly see themselves as the "head nation" and who use "head" lotions will in fact be at the "head" of those who go into captivity. A none too subtle warning is given to all who blindly think of themselves as number one.

Amos goes on to ask, "Are Israel and Judah better than the nearby nations they have subjugated?" (see verse 2). The implied answer is clearly "No"! Israel has no right to think herself better than other nations. By so doing, she has gravely misinterpreted her standing before Yahweh. He is more interested in justice and righteousness than vain thoughts of importance. Israel needs her eyes opened to her true situation before God.

The reason for this exile is clearly outlined in verses 4-6. These particular Israelites are living very well! They rest on expensive beds inlaid with ivory. They have lots of free time to lounge and play music. They don't need to work as others do. They dine on choice lambs and fatted calves when most Israelites probably eat meat only a few times a year at festivals. Instead of drinking wine from goblets, as is normal, they have so much to consume that they drink out of large bowls. The picture is one of conspicuous consumption and flagrant leisure. All that, however, is not really the bottom line.

What concerns Amos and God in this case is not Israel's obvious wealth and attendant laziness, but their complacency. These rich Israelites do not "grieve over the ruin of Joseph" (vs 6b). The terrible injustices done and the oppression of one group of God's people by another part of God's people has not concerned them. They don't mourn, and they don't care. This is what galls Amos. Israel's elite looked evil in the eye and did not even see it. They simply went on blindly enjoying wealth and pleasure.

Amos and God are not through yet. There remains one more "woe" in verses 8-14. God detests Israel's pride, particularly as manifested in its fortresses. Pride is shown in military self-confidence. Israel has more trust in her fortifications than in God. How misplaced that confidence is! The Lord has decreed such fortresses will be smashed into bits and Israel will be taken over by a foreign nation and oppressed.

Israel (and *we!*) should find such a section stunning. The three sins mentioned here are not what one would normally expect in a catalog of major sins. No murder, adultery, idolatry, or theft are found. The people who are condemned appear religious. They are rich, which in ancient near-eastern culture was a sign of God's blessing. Military security appears to be in place. What could be wrong with such people? According to Amos, their religion is a form, their wealth leads to unconcern for the poor, and their military makes them proud and self-sufficient. What appears to be right all turns out to be very, very wrong. Sin is deceptive, and outward appearances deceive. We need to ask ourselves if we may exhibit some of these same sins.

Five Symbols of Judgment

This next section of Amos continues the judgment theme, conveying it by means of five visual images or visions. These five visions are:

1. *Swarms of locusts* that come up and strip the land clean (7:1-3).
2. *Fire* that dries up water and land (vss. 4-6).
3. *A plumb line* that shows the "building" of God's people is nei-

ther true nor straight (vss. 7-9).

4. *A basket of ripe fruit* that shows the time is right for God's people to be "picked" (8:1-14).

5. *The Lord Himself standing by the altar* and causing the temple to fall down in judgment on the people (9:1-10).

The first two visions of judgment have amazing endings. In fact, Amos is so overcome by the threat of what this judgment will do that he cries out to God for mercy. He says, "How can Jacob survive? He is so small!" (7:2, 5).

In the first vision, the locusts that strip the land clean arrive *after* the king's straw had been harvested, but before the second crop. Evidently, the first cutting of the pastures paid royal taxes, while the second was for the people. Amos couldn't bear the thought that the king got his share, but the people would have nothing.

The fire of the second vision could well represent drought, which leads to famine. Amos can't bear to think of his people going hungry. For a farmer, as Amos was, these two punishments probably seemed particularly vivid and horrible. His heart goes out to his people, so he asks God to forgive them.

God does "relent" (NIV) or "repent" (KJV, RSV) or as Today's English Version says, "changes His mind." The promised judgment "will not happen" (vss. 3, 6). The two promised judgments are not simply postponed, but in fact canceled.

When the Bible speaks of God repenting, it is not a statement that God needs to get rid of sin. Rather, it is referring to God's willingness to change. Amos is not the only Old Testament writer to make such statements (see Exod. 32:12, 14; Jer. 18:8-10; 26:19). What is the significance of such teaching?

First, this idea says some things about Amos. When we read all of his judgment sermons, it would be easy to get the idea that Amos didn't care about Israel. These verses make it clear that Amos was deeply concerned about Israel. These statements in Amos 7 leave the impression that Amos acted almost instinctively with his heart and emotions against the locusts and fire. His is not some considered, reflected on, dutiful response, but the spontaneous reaction of someone with real compassion.

Second, Amos must have been a powerful interceder. In reality, his intercessory prayer saves Israel from threatened judgment. Much like Moses, who reaches out to God to save his people (Exod. 33:12-17), Amos pleads for his endangered people and secures their deliverance. What an example these men give of intercessory prayer by religious leaders for the people entrusted to their care! Not only does this passage make clear Amos's mercy and care, but it also emphasizes the grace of Yahweh. Knowing the judgment in this book, the casual reader could come to see God as cruel and even vindictive. Not so! God does not delight in judgment, but rather seems quite willing to forgive and forget. Judgment, in the book of Amos, is not a gleeful, pay-you-back kind of thing, but the reluctant judgment of a grieved and merciful God.

The biggest problem some people have with these statements, however, is the idea that God changes His mind. Does this not imply God may have been wrong? Some even quote Malachi 3:6, "I the Lord do not change." How do you put together the relenting, changing God of Amos and the changeless God of Malachi?

God's basic nature and character are changeless, which is the main point of Malachi 3:6. God *always* loves His people. Based on that love, God acts in a dynamic relationship with humans. He actually listens and responds to them and their prayers. That is Amos's point. God's unchanging love is acted out in different ways that may even include changing His mind in a true give-and-take interchange.

If this is the case, we must be careful how we explain the attributes of God. Many people misunderstand what I call the "omni's." Many of us were taught that God is *omni*present (present everywhere), *omni*scient (all knowing), *omni*potent (all powerful)—and immutable (unchanging). My study of Amos and the Old Testament teaches me that these "omni's" are true, but not in an absolute sense. God must also be seen in a dynamic relationship with people. Omniscience and immutability have to be understood in a way that allows for God to relent, change His mind, and give conditional prophecies.

I personally believe that the idea that Yahweh relents from judgment on the basis of intercession is good news. It is good news because it tells us about the real involvement of God with people where they truly are in life, and it is good news because it tells us about the power of prayer.

When we reach the vision of the plumb line, the mood changes (7:7-9). Amos does not intercede, and God specifically states that He can spare "My people Israel . . . no longer." God still cares, because the people are clearly-termed "my people," but sin must be dealt with eventually.

Note also that the judgment mentioned here is much more narrow and specific than are the fire and the locusts. The plumb-line judgment affects the high places, the sanctuaries of Israel, and the royal house of Jeroboam only—avoiding the universal effect of the first two visions and dealing only with the specific places and people involved in sin.

This third vision leads directly to Amos's encounter with Amaziah. As priest at Bethel, the major northern sanctuary, Amaziah is directly affected by the plumb-line vision, which foretells the ruin of the northern sanctuaries. Such a sanctuary would be under royal sponsorship and direction. Mention of Jeroboam's dynasty also directly concerns Amaziah. Amaziah is upset and angry.

Amaziah's first act is to report the matter to Jeroboam, the king and his boss. Although the book of Amos has not said so, Amaziah makes it clear Amos has been preaching at Bethel (7:13). He may have spoken his words against the sanctuaries of Israel right at the main royal sanctuary of Bethel!

In his report to Jeroboam, Amaziah accuses Amos of raising a conspiracy against Jeroboam (vs. 10). This seems to be both untrue and misleading. Amos is condemning Israel's sins, not necessarily seeking to dethrone Jeroboam. In his desire to get rid of Amos, Amaziah, in his message to Jeroboam, says and does at least three more things that are either false or misleading.

First, Amaziah reports that *Amos* is saying certain things (vs. 11). The prophet has attempted to make it clear that the words he speaks are not his, but Yahweh's. Amaziah, by his very introductory words, warps what Amos is claiming—to be God's mouthpiece.

Second, Amos is portrayed as saying that Jeroboam will die by the sword (vs. 11). Nowhere in his book does Amos say this. Amaziah goes beyond anything Amos has said and deliberately tries to arouse the king.

Third, Amaziah nowhere gives the rationale for Amos's words. Amos always declares Israel's sin to be a reason for God's judgment. Omitting this context for Amos's words misleads the king into viewing the prophet as a gadabout troublemaker, rather than one who points out sin and its consequences.

After his message to the king, Amaziah orders Amos deported back to Judah. He can no longer prophesy at Bethel (vs. 13). Amaziah does this with a sneer and a smear. Amos, he says, is to earn his bread and prophesy in Judah (vs. 12). The implied accusation is that Amos has been prophesying at Bethel and making big money at it. He should earn his living in Judah. This is the reason for the first part of Amos's reply: "I was neither a prophet nor a prophet's son, but I was a shepherd" (vs. 14). The best way to understand what Amos is saying is to place the word *paid* or *professional* in front of the word *prophet*. Amos knows he is a prophet and a spokesman for God, but he is not a prophet *for hire*. Over a period of time, the schools of the prophets and the prophetic guides had, in some places, become corrupt. False prophets abounded (see, for example, Jer. 23:9-40). These "prophets" made their money prophesying good things. Amaziah has implied that Amos is one of these types. Amos denies the charge vehemently. He supports himself, he declares, by agricultural work, not prophecy!

Amos goes on to describe his divine call (7:15) and then to demonstrate it (vs. 16). God chose him and took him away from the flock and commanded him to go and prophesy to Israel. Now he demonstrates that call by proclaiming God's word to Amaziah. What is that word?

Amos directly condemns Amaziah in stark terms (vs. 17). His wife will become a prostitute in the city—probably Bethel. The implication seems to be that she will need to do this to support herself. His sons and daughters will be killed. The land of Israel (or perhaps his personal property) will be given to another, and he himself will die in exile.

Although graphic, these curses are typical of covenant curses. By forbidding Amos to prophesy, Amaziah has gone against God and His command. These future consequences in Amaziah's life are some of the results outlined in the covenant curses (see Deut. 28:30; 32:25). As a conclusion, Amos reiterates the approaching exile of Israel. We do not know from Scripture what Amaziah's reaction was to all this, but I doubt he slept well for at least several nights!

The fourth vision is of a basket of ripe fruit (Amos 8:1, 2). Amos is asked to identify what God shows him, and he readily does. That poses no problem for an old fruit farmer and a fig-slitter such as Amos. God shows Amos a vision that he can easily relate to.

The NIV translation of this passage obscures the clever literary devise used in Hebrew. The Hebrew words for *fruit* and *end* are written almost identically. In the northern kingdom of Amos's time, these two words were pronounced identically—*qetz* (Stuart, 379). The phrase in verse 2 (NIV), "The time is ripe," could better be translated "the end has come." The *qetz* (fruit) Amos sees in the basket is to remind him that the *qetz* (end) has come for Israel.

Yahweh's interpretation of the vision clearly has to do with time. Not only has the end come, but Yahweh declares, "I will spare them no longer" (vs. 2). In the first two visions, Yahweh relents, and nothing happens. In the third vision, the destruction of Israel and her exile are foretold. In this fourth vision, *time* is the key.

This time context is the basis for the continual reference to "that day" in the rest of the passage (see vss. 3, 9, 13) and also for the phrase, "the days are coming" (vs. 11). What God has foretold about Israel's exile, Amos declares, will happen very soon.

In the process of outlining what will happen at the time of the end, this fourth vision reiterates and enlarges the specific charges against Israel. Remember, judgment oracles almost *always* give reasons for judgment. We have already seen the charges of trampling on the poor (vs. 4) and illicit slavery (vs. 6). Verse 5 brings forth a new charge.

In form, Israel strictly keeps the new moon and Sabbath. But as soon as the Sabbath ends, the people go back to business. Business as usual, for them, involves cheating. They skimp on the amount sold, boost the price, and use dishonest scales. In Israel, we are confronted with strict seventh-day Sabbath keepers who are corrupt business people. Why do they keep the part of the law that forbids commerce on Sabbath and neglect the part of the law that expressly forbids dishonest business practices (Lev. 19:35, 36; Deut. 25:13-15)? We must say that they are *selective* law keepers. They keep the religious form but don't follow the ethical meaning. The passage implies that God "hates" their Sabbath keeping, just as He hates their religious feasts and assemblies (Amos 5:21).

How does the Lord respond to this? He swears a solemn oath, that is, He makes an irrevocable commitment to a certain course of action (8:7). He "will never forget anything they have done" (vs 7). The poor, the slaves, and the cheated have a dedicated and determined protector in the God of Israel. That protector is about to execute judgment because of this despicable behavior.

In the outline of the judgment that follows, two things should be especially noticed. First, verse 9 portrays the judgment with typical "day of the Lord" language. The sun is affected—and probably other heavenly bodies as well. We have already seen such portrayals in Joel (2:2, 31) and should recognize that such terms are used by other prophets also (see, for example, Isa. 8:22; Zeph. 1:15). It also seems to be hinted at in the covenant curse found in Deuteronomy 28:29 where people are portrayed as groping in the dark.

Second, Amos 8:11, 12 proclaim a particular kind of famine that will come. This is a famine of hearing the words of Yahweh. People will search from sea to sea (probably meaning from the Mediterranean to the Dead Sea) and north to east and not be able to hear the word. In other words, the whole country will be without prophetic revelation. This is a tragedy, for the law says this word is vital to life (Deut. 8:3). People will seek to hear from God, but they will be answered by silence. For people desperate to know the meaning of what is happening, this is horrible. The final results of this false Sabbath keeping are terrible.

In the fifth, and last, vision (9:1-10), the final step in the sequence of judgment is taken. Yahweh Himself stands by the altar in the temple, His dwelling, and performs His judgment acts.

Judgment is finally executed.

In summary, the progression of judgment, as portrayed in these five visions, follows this path:

1. *Judgment is deferred.* Although God proclaims destruction in the first two visions, He responds in mercy to the intercessory pleas of Amos and relents.

2. *Judgment is declared.* In the third vision, Israel's exile is foretold, and objections to it are overcome.

3. *Judgment is scheduled.* In the fourth vision, the judgment is not delayed. The end has come, and time is short.

4. *Judgment is executed.* In the fifth vision, God Himself performs the act of destruction that has been foretold. With this, the cycle of judgment is complete, and we can look ahead to restoration.

God Restores Israel

Amos concludes with a promise of restoration. To understand the promise fully, we need to look at the latter part of the final judgment oracle—especially 9:7-10.

God clearly says He is the Lord of the Cushites (Ethiopians), Egyptians, Philistines, and Arameans as well as the God of Israel (vs. 7). In other words, Israel is not special simply because God controls her history; God works in the history of *all* nations. God can, and will, judge any sinful kingdom (vs. 8). His destruction of Israel, how-ever, will *not* be total (vs. 8b). Specifically, God will deal with sinners among His people and with those who refuse to believe in His judg-ment (vs. 10).

This is crucial for two reasons. First, the reiteration of God's sov-ereign rule over *all* nations forms a background for the restoration. God can restore Israel, and God can subjugate Israel's neighbors, because He is Lord of history; that is His business.

Second, most of the book of Amos seems to speak of God's judg-ment in general, universal terms. *All* Israel is to be judged. Even in chapter 9 itself, this is stated: "*Not one* will get away, *none* will es-cape" (vs. 1, emphasis supplied) and "*all*" will mourn (vs. 5). The final word, however, is that *sinners* die (vs. 10), so, in reality, not all die—only sinners receive judgment. It is clear in the earlier part of the book that it is speaking of judgment in broad, general terms. There is, however, an exception—the righteous! Only sinners die. For most people, that puts the whole matter in a new light. A remnant will be spared. Judgment applies to the sinners, *not* the righteous.

In that case, restoration makes sense. Salvation must logically come for the righteous remnant and so Amos proclaims it.

The promises of restoration cover three main areas: (1) Israel's enemies are overcome (vss. 11, 12); (2) agricultural prosperity is restored (vs. 13); and (3) finally Israel is able to repossess, rebuild, and restore her cities and land (vss. 14, 15).

Part of phase one of this restoration is the promise that David's "tent," or dynasty, will be restored. This dynasty will rule over the nations that were formerly part of the larger, united Isarel ("the nations that bear my name," vs. 12b). This seems to imply the fulfillment of the promises that God gave to both Abraham and David. Jews have traditionally seen this passage as messianic!

Just as interesting as the restoration promises that have been stated are the things that have not been stated. Nowhere does the passage outline Israel's power or ability to bring about restoration. Israel is not told to do something first. The restoration is an act of God's power and grace. Israel could not do it in her own strength or might. Only God can bring this about. The people have only to receive it. God acts on behalf of His people who have seen their need and who have turned to Him for help.

The time period for all of this is a rather general "in that day" (vs. 11a). Historically, it does not seem that this prophecy was fulfilled to the literal nothern kingdom. The position I have taken is that such promises now apply in general to God's people (spiritual Israel), because literal Israel failed to respond to God's message. (See the Introduction to this volume for a fuller explanation.)

What is most important for us to realize about Amos's message is God's good intentions. This is what He *really wanted* for Israel. His thoughts and desires for her were good continually. His final word is not destruction, but deliverance. His final aim is not lasting death, but full life. He wounds that He may heal. Even a book as full of judgment and destruction as is Amos places God's real, final aim of salvation as the last word.

▪ Applying the Word

Amos 5:18–9:15

1. Can you think of situations in the world or in the church today that are so serious that we should sing or play funeral songs over them as Amos did? If so, list these in your notebook. What kind of music or words would you use? How would you get the message across?
2. J. Elliot Corbett, in his book *The Prophets on Main Street* applies two portions of Amos we have studied to a modern setting.

THE VENEER OF PIETY (5:21-24)

I hate your new church buildings,
    I take no great pleasure in your rising membership rolls.
The tinkle of your treasuries give me an earache!
    Take away from my sight your veneer of piety.
To your boasts of being a Christian nation I will not listen.
But let justice roll down like waters,
    And righteousness like an ever-flowing stream.

IDLE IRRESPONSIBILITY (6:4-7)

Hear this word, you who while away the idle hours, saying,
    "When will the next bingo game be played?" or
    "What club shall we go to tonight?"
Woe unto you who go to deep freezers, saying,
    "Shall it be steak or chicken?"
    but care little for my children in India who have no rice.
For I will take away what you think you have,
    and give it to those who have none.

Do you agree, or disagree, with these attempts to give modern applications to the message of Amos? Why? If not, how would you apply these passages today?

3. Amos has very strong feelings about those who follow religious forms and have outward piety, but are not just and fair to their fellowmen. Do you see examples of this same situation today? List these. Have you ever been guilty of this in your own life?

4. Are complacency and pride still problem sins today? Why? How are they manifested in our country, church, and lives? If Amos were alive today, what sins do you think he would point out in the church? What is the problem with relying on material things or military might for security?

5. How do you relate to the idea of God repenting or relenting? Does God still do that today? When? How? Has He done it in your life? How? Does the idea give you joy or scare you? Why?

6. Amos condemns Sabbath keepers who are dishonest in business. Do you know of any today? How does this text apply today? Does a Sabbath keeper who cheats on his tax, or pays his employees unfairly, receive God's condemnation? Is it any real benefit for such a person to keep the Sabbath if he continues his injustice? Why, or why not?

7. Is there a famine today for the Word of the Lord? Give a reason for your answer. Is there a way to solve the problem if it exists? Are there words today from God that come to us from outside the Scripture? What are they? Do you think if we sinned less God would send His Word to us more often?

■ Researching the Word

1. Amos 8:5 mentions the new moon festival. Use a concordance to find out all you can about this festival, including its history and observance. Some texts to start with are Numbers 10:10; 28:11; 1 Samuel 20:24, 25; 2 Kings 4:23; Isaiah 1:13; Hosea 2:11. Compare your findings with those in a Bible dictionary. Why did Amos mention the new moon fes-

tival in the same verse with the Sabbath?

2. Amos 9:7 mentions three interesting names and places that are not too well known—Cushite, Caphtor, and Kir. Use a Bible dictionary to find out what these names refer to. Use an atlas to find out where Cush, Caphtor, and Kir are. Did the Philistines come from Caphtor and the Arameans from Kir? If so, how did they get to their locations in the time of Amos?

∎ Further Study of the Word

1. For interesting information on how the rich and high-society people lived in Amos's time, see King, *Amos, Hosea, Micah*, 137-161.
2. To find out more about the ivory inlaid beds mentioned in Amos 6:4, see Thompson, *Handbook of Life in Bible Times*, 196, 197, which explains ivory carving in Bible times.
3. In several places Amos speaks against the abuse of slavery. To find out more about slaves in Old Testament times, see De Vaux, *Ancient Israel*, 1:80-90.

PART FOUR

Obadiah

Arrogant Edom
Falls

CHAPTER TEN

Introduction
to Obadiah

Obadiah's one chapter, with only twenty-one verses, makes it the shortest book in the Old Testament. If the book makes anything clear, it is that God cares about what happens in Gentile nations—in this case, the little country of Edom that lay south and east of Israel.

The closest parallel to the book of Obadiah is the slightly longer book of Nahum, which deals with the judgment of another single Gentile nation— Assyria and its capital of Nineveh.

Although Edom was a fairly insignificant nation in the larger sense, it was important in relationship to Israel. In fact, the prophets spoke against Edom on a broader scale than they did against any other nation outside the "big three"—Egypt, Assyria, and Babylon. Isaiah (11:14; 21:11, 12), Jeremiah (25:21; 49:7-22), and Ezekiel (25:12-14; 35) all deal at length with Edom. Among the shorter prophetic books, Amos (1:11, 12) and Malachi (1:2-5) as well as Obadiah prophesy against this mountain kingdom—as does Lamentations (4:21). In the prophets' eyes, Edom was crucial. Obadiah is clearly not alone in his deep concern about the behavior of this small nation. As our study proceeds, we will find out why this is so.

■ Getting Into the Word

Read Obadiah through twice. It won't take long! As you read, look for answers to the following questions:

1. What is Obadiah trying to say? Why did he write his book?

How would you summarize his message in one sentence?
Try to understand the basic message of the book.
2. If you were a Jew reading the book, how would it affect you?
Would it encourage you? Why, or why not? What would you
learn about your God from the book?

Obadiah the Man

The name *Obadiah* means "servant of Yahweh" or "worshiper of
Yahweh" (*Obed*=servant; *iah*=shortened form of the divine name,
Yahweh). Some have suggested that this name is like the "name"
Malachi (meaning "My messenger") and is really a title rather than a
name. This is probably not true, since many Old Testament charac-
ters bear this name. Thirteen different Obadiahs are mentioned from
Davidic to postexilic times (Stuart, 406). In addition, there are six
persons including David's grandfather, who bear the name Obed,
which is probably a shortened form of the same name.

The book tells us nothing directly about the author. His father is
not even mentioned. The Jewish Babylonian Talmud identifies this
Obadiah as the same Obadiah who worked for King Ahab (1 Kings
18:3-16). Most scholars today reject this identification as unlikely.

We can tell indirectly from his book that Obadiah possessed literary skills that fit his calling. Not only was he good at Hebrew poetic
parallelism, but he had a facility for imagery, rhetorical questions,
irony, and repetition.

Historical Setting

For such a small book, the historical questions relating to it are
large. There exists no consensus as to when the book was written,
and the range of suggested possibilities is vast.

What is clear from the book is that Obadiah makes reference to
an incident in history when Edom mistreated Israel (10-14). Edom
is pictured as allowing strangers to plunder Jerusalem and even participating with them (11, 12). She goes so far as to cut down Jewish
fugitives and hand over survivors to the enemy (14). The issue is:

When did this happen? Suggestions range from preexilic times (especially the later half of the ninth century B.C.) through the early exilic period (mid-sixth century) to postexilic, or fourth- and fifth-century B.C. times (McComiskey II, 496, 497).

The two most popular views are that this incident happened either in the time of Jehoram (852–841 B.C.—see 2 Kings 8:16-24 and 2 Chron. 21:4-20) or during the time of the Babylonian invasions culminating in 586 B.C. with the fall of Jerusalem. Both dates have circumstances that could give rise to the statement in the book. I agree that the similarity of Obadiah's description to that of Jeremiah (49:7-22) and Ezekiel (25:12-14; 35) seem to imply the latter date. For a strong defense of the Jehoram date, see McComiskey (McComiskey, II:496-502). We will assume the later date in our comments on the text.

Theme and Message

Although Obadiah addresses Edom, the book would not be preserved in the Old Testament if it had not said something to Israel. For Israel, the theme is clearly *hope*. The Israelites may be oppressed, downtrodden, and beat up, but those who have misused them will be judged. Edom will not get away free of consequences after its violence to Israel. God is still sovereign over history and will intercede on behalf of His people.

Justice is also a theme. When people sin against others, they do not forever escape. The day of payback will come. Compensatory judgment is promised.

The question still rises—why pick on Edom? At least three reasons exist (Stuart, 404):

1. The sheer *chronological length* of the enmity is amazing. Edom is seen, of course, as the nation stemming from Esau. The struggle between Esau and Jacob goes back to the womb (see Gen. 25) and the very earliest era of Israel. As a nation, Edom was Israel's enemy from the early period just after the Exodus to the later period after the exile.

2. The enmity seems to have been vindictive (Obad. 10-14). Edom was not just defending itself, but was actually looking for ways to take advantage of and mistreat Israel.

3. Edom (Esau) was a "brother." Realizing how extremely important kinship is in Semitic society, it was especially galling to Israelites to have a close relative treat them so badly (see Amos 1:11—"his brother").

This helps us understand why Edom was singled out and why it played such a crucial role in the mind of Israel at that time.

Outline of Obadiah
Arrogant Edom Falls

I. Title and Introduction (1)
II. Edom judged (2-14)
  A. Judgment pronounced (2-9)
  B. Reasons for judgment (10-14)
III. The day of the lord (15-21)
  A. Nations judged (15, 16)
  B. Israel delivered (17-21)

CHAPTER ELEVEN

Arrogant Edom Falls

Obadiah 1-21

Since the book of Obadiah will be covered in one short chapter in this book, the general Introduction serves also as the introduction to this chapter. Reread it if you wish!

■ Getting Into the Word

Obadiah 1-21

1. Edom was viewed by Obadiah as a nation that was "high." Note carefully, and then list, all the references in this book that mention or allude to this fact. How does Obadiah use this theme to help communicate his message?
2. List the specific things God says will come upon Edom. In verses 15 and 16, God addresses the nations in general. What does He say will happen to them? How does their judgment compare with the judgment on Edom? How do you account for the difference?
3. We have seen the day-of-the-Lord concept used in both Joel and Amos. How does Obadiah's idea of the meaning of the day of the Lord (vss. 15-21) compare with the concepts presented by the other two prophets? How does Obadiah's emphasis differ from theirs?
4. List the promises God makes to His people in Obadiah. On

what are the promises based? How do these promises fit
with the theme of the book of Obadiah and its historical
situation?

■ Exploring the Word

Judgment on Edom

In common with many prophetic books, Obadiah refers to his
message as "the vision" (vs. 1). Some actually translate the word as
"revelation" (Allen, *The Books of Joel, Obadiah, Jonah, and Micah*, 144),
since the word means "a divine communication." Because many prophetic revelations did occur by means of a vision, this term is an
appropriate one, even though God gave the message to Obadiah in
words rather then in pictures. The claim that Obadiah received his
message by divine revelation is further strengthened by the second
and third sentences in verse 1, which specifically point out that the
speaker is not Obadiah, but rather the "Sovereign Lord." The message about Edom comes from Israel's God.

Obadiah goes on to say, "We have heard a message from the Lord"
(vs. 1). It could be an editorial "we." It could even possibly be referring to other prophetic declarations about Edom. But most likely it
shows the prophet's association and identification with Israel. Strictly
speaking, the message is from Obadiah, but he is a representative of
the people, and the message is for all of them. God's revelations are
not merely personal for the prophet, but corporate for the whole
nation.

Who is this Edom that is the subject of the divine message? Edom,
also called Seir (see Gen. 32:3; 36:20, 21, 31; Num. 24:18), lay south
and east of Israel and the Dead Sea. The name Edom means "red,"
which is appropriate because the progenitor of Edom, Esau, as a
baby emerged red (see Gen. 25:25). A red-colored sandstone was
also found throughout Edom. Edomite territory was roughly one
hundred miles long (north to south) and averaged about sixty miles
in width.

During Bible times, two major trade routes passed through

Edom—the king's highway and the road along the Arabah (the rift valley between the Dead Sea and the Red Sea). These north-south trade roads fed Edom's coffers and opened it to attack by jealous enemies. At this point, it would be helpful to consult the maps in the back of your Bible.

In Bible times, the heart of Edom lay east of this Arabah rift valley where the land rose rather sharply from the valley and formed a rugged mountainous area with peaks of 3,500 feet and higher.

Sela (literally "crag" or "rock" in Hebrew), the capital and fortress city, was on a massive rocky plateau that towers 1,000 feet above the present-day Petra (the Greek translation of Sela). The plateau is about 3,700 feet above sea level. (Please note that Petra and the famous "red city" that people visit today in Palestine is in the former territory of biblical Edom but was built by the Nabateans during a later period beginning in the fourth century B.C.)

A knowledge of Edom's mountainous terrain helps explain all the references in Obadiah to heights and mountains and to the "bringing down" of the nation. Edom lives "in the clefts of the rocks" and makes her "home on the heights" (vs. 3). She doesn't think anyone can bring her "down to the ground" (vs. 3). Edom soars like an eagle and makes her nest among the "stars," but from there God will bring her "down" (vs. 4). Other similar references include "the mountains of Esau" (vs. 8, 9, 21) or "Esau's mountains" whose inhabitants will be "cut down" (vs. 9).

I believe Obadiah also uses these references in a figurative sense. The initial accusation against Edom is her pride and arrogance. She speaks and thinks "highly" of herself (vs. 3). God is about to make her small (short?) among the nation (vs. 2). The bringing down to the ground spoken of in verses 3b and 4 seems to have a double meaning. Edom will be literally brought down from her mountain strongholds, but spiritually and attitudinally she will be brought down from her high and haughty pride as well. She will no longer be able to "look down" on her brothers when she is judged.

Sela could be approached only from the southeast. All other approaches were perpendicular cliff-walls. From the easy-to-defend fortress, Edom looked down on everyone, both literally and figuratively. Under God's judgment, this "highness" will be dealt with in all its aspects, and the lofty will become low.

What exactly is God going to do in His judgment on Edom? What does it mean to be brought low? Besides the general statement that Edom will be made small or brought down, what specifically is in store for her?

Her fate includes military conquest and subsequent pillaging, slavery, and slaughter. Edom will be ransacked and her hidden treasures pillaged (vs. 6). Edom's supposed allies will prove treacherous, and those she thought were her friends will deceive and entrap her (vs. 7). All classes of people will be destroyed, including her wise men and warriors that some might think would escape (8, 9). Edom will end up with no survivors (vs. 18), and others will take her land (vss. 19-21).

This description is particularly instructive when it talks of the treachery of Edom's allies (vs. 7). While talk of conquest, plunder, slavery, and death is common in judgment passages, verse 7 talks of something unique. Those who are closest to Edom and should have helped her, turn on her, and she is unknowingly trapped.

The irony of the situation is clear. Edom's pride is particularly manifested in violence against her "brother Jacob" (vs. 10). The nation of Israel was Edom's (Esau's) brother. Edom should have been an ally to her "brother" Israel, but instead she has proven treacherous and has helped the enemies of God's people to plunder Jerusalem. She should not have looked down on her "brother" (vs. 12) this way. "Now," Yahweh says, "the same thing will happen to you, Edom. Those closest to you will betray you. Your brother nations will contribute to your downfall."

While God is quite specific in His judgment on Edom, He is general in His portrayal of judgment on the other nations (vss. 15, 16). The general principle of God's judgment, which is illustrated by Edom, is stated simply:

> As you have done, it will be done to you;
> your deeds will return upon your own head (vs. 15).

The next verse (vs. 16) illustrates the principle—as Edom and the other nations have drunk and caroused on God's holy hill (Jerusalem), so God will give them to drink the cup of His judgment (Psa. 75:8, 9). They will drink and drink until they will be as if they had never been. Christians cannot help but think of the words of Jesus as He shrank in Gethsemane from the cup of God's judgment on sin, but nevertheless asked to follow God's will for Him (Mark 14:36).

The basic principle of judgment stated here and illustrated in the experience of Edom is often called *lex talionis* (Latin for "law of retaliation"). This law harks back to Exodus 21:23, 24 that speaks of life being given for life, eye for eye, and tooth for tooth. For many people, this law has a negative connotation that I believe is undeserved. Part of this negative image may stem from its name—"law of retaliation." But this is really not a law of retaliation. Rather, it is one that says the judgment or punishment should correspond to, and be appropriate to, the crime. Isn't this better than a punishment that does *not* fit the crime?

When Jesus speaks against this law in Matthew 5:38-42, He does so in the context of a willingness to forgive wrongs rather than exacting judgment. We must remember that Yahweh in the Old Testament is also willing to forgive. Remember, for example, our recent study in Amos 7:1-6. Jesus rightly encourages us to follow this example. Even the New Testament, however, portrays a day of judgment and final reckoning. In that day, we must believe that God's judgment corresponds to the sin or wrong. We would not want to serve a God who operated by any other principle. The principle is clearly stated here in Obadiah because God wants Edom and the nations to know that He is just and fair. He wants us to realize the same thing too.

The Day of the Lord

Besides the two major themes of height/pride and *lex talionis*/justice, there is a third theme that comes through in the book of Obadiah. That theme is "day."

Edom can look forward to "that day" (vs. 8) when God will judge all her people because of "the day" (vs. 11) when she stood aloof at Jerusalem's plunder and looked down on her brother on the "day" of his misfortune (vss. 12-14). For that reason, "the day of the Lord" for all nations is near (vs. 15). In an earlier *day* when Israel was in trouble, Edom stood by and even contributed to her downfall. Likewise, a *day* will come for Edom and the nations when they will meet their judgment.

We are already somewhat familiar with the day-of-the-Lord concepts in Joel and Amos. Joel gives a quite comprehensive view of the day of the Lord, portraying both the positive, saving aspect of the day, as well as the negative side of judgment. For Joel, the day affects both Israel and the nation. Amos, through a heavy emphasis on Israel's judgment, attempts to correct a view that saw the day as only a saving time for Israel. Amos sees the day as a day of darkness and loss for Israel.

Obadiah's treatment of the day of the Lord is closer to Joel's emphasis than to that of Amos. Obadiah's interest in Edom fits with his portrayal of the day of the Lord as a day of judgment on the nations (vs. 15), in particular the nation of His special concern, Edom (vs. 18). The day, however, is also a time of deliverance for Mount Zion and the house of Jacob (vs. 17). The only significant difference between Joel and Obadiah is the time frame. Joel, as mentioned earlier, seems to see the visitation of the Lord in two stages—an earlier locust plague with a later visitation (Joel 2:28—"afterward"). Obadiah seems to see a one-phase day of the Lord that is "near" (vs. 15).

I see no real contradictions between the three portrayals. Joel's is the most complete picture and furnishes the basic outline, while the other two prophets give only partial pictures. Amos deals only with the negative aspect of the day. Obadiah portrays both the judging and the saving aspects of the day but does not develop a full time sequence. Both Amos and Obadiah talk about those parts of the day of the Lord that apply to the message they want to get across.

What promises does God make to His people in the context of the day of the Lord? He promises that Mount Zion will be delivered and that the house of Jacob will possess its inheritance (vs. 17). The clear implication is that Jerusalem has either been captured or is under attack or siege and that Jacob (Israel) is in danger of losing its land. In both cases, God will save and help His people.

Israel will also be empowered to destroy Edom, leaving no survivors (vs. 18). Territory that once belonged to Edom and the Philistines will be taken over (vss. 19a, 21a). The people who get these lands are not specifically identified but probably are the remnant of Israel. These last three verses portray Israel as not only possessing her own land, but that of her neighbors as well. In the end, the final word is that the kingdom will be the Lord's.

Obadiah has discussed the interplay of nations and peoples; now, in conclusion, it is time to affirm who really is in control. Yahweh, the Lord, rules the kingdom—not any other god or any other king or nation. Yahweh alone is sovereign over His people.

As is so often true in the prophets, no human being or decision is mentioned as a basis for God's action. There is no repentance, prayer, or other factor given as a cause other than the gracious delivering act of God. Edom has been a terrible problem for God's people, but God takes care of that problem Himself. No longer will Edom possess Israel. Instead, Israel will take over and possess Edom because of Israel's God. In the end, Obadiah is not simply the story of ancient Edom and ancient Israel. Obadiah is the story of God's enemies, God's people, and the work of God on behalf of His own. That story is relevant to every age, including our own. Whatever "Edom" may be afflicting us, the same God acts to deliver His people now as He did then.

■ Applying the Word

Obadiah 1-21

1. **What nations, ethnic or religious groups, or individuals today, like Edom, indulge in pride and see themselves as "high"? How do you respond to such groups or individuals? Why? Could such individuals or groups be brought down? How? What would be the proper way to help them see their pride and change?**

2. Do you think God still operates today by the principle "as you have done, it will be done to you" (vs. 15)? If so, does this principle apply to groups or individuals or both? Give reasons for your answer. What other ways or principles are there by which God acts? How should God judge people?

3. Edom was Israel's "brother" and thus had special responsibilities. Does God still hold us especially responsible to those who are closely related to us? Who would such people be for us as individuals, as a church, and as a nation? How should we relate?

4. Edom was judged by God for responding improperly to Israel's crisis of foreign invasion. How do we respond when our enemies suffer misfortune? Do we rejoice? Or do we show pity and help them? What should we do when others face crises and problems? How can we avoid a judgment similar to Edom's?

■ Researching the Word

1. Compare the prophecy of Obadiah with Jeremiah 49:7-22, which also talks about Edom. What similarities and differences do you see? Some have seen Jeremiah as using Obadiah, and some see the opposite. Others see no direct connection. What do you think? Why?

2. Use a Bible dictionary or encyclopedia and an atlas to find out as much about Edom and its capital Teman as possible. List some of the facts you find that help you understand this book of Obadiah better.

■ Further Study of the Word

1. For general background on an earlier encounter between Edom and Israel, see E. G. White, *Patriarchs and Prophets*, 422-425. For background on Esau, see pages 207-209.

2. For a detailed introduction to the prophet and prophecy of Obadiah, see LaSor, et al., *Old Testament Survey*, 455-460.

PART FIVE

Jonah

God's
Missionary Heart

CHAPTER TWELVE

Introduction to Jonah

Jonah is a unique book. Not only is Jonah different from the other prophets we study in this volume, but his book is also different from any other Old Testament book. Because of these differences, Jonah is, in my estimation, the most miraculous book in the Bible. Let me explain—first the uniqueness and then the miraculousness of Jonah's book.

All the other prophetic books we are studying consist mainly of oracles— that is, messages from God delivered by the prophet. These messages are usually couched in poetic language. In contrast, Jonah is a story. All the other prophets appear in a good light. They may not always be popular with the people, but they are seen as righteous people who speak for God. Jonah is a villain. He, the prophet, is portrayed in a bad light. He runs away from God and tries to avoid God's call.

Among the twelve "minor prophets," Jonah is the only one whom God sends to minister in a foreign land. Obadiah may prophesy about Edom, but he does not "work" there. The other prophets clearly minister to Israel or Judah. Outside of a few isolated cases, we know little about the success or failure of other prophets. Jonah's preaching is successful almost beyond be-lief, yet he is disturbed by that success! Jonah is different—even from evan-gelists today!

All of this makes it miraculous to me that the book not only has been preserved by the Jews, but that it even has found a place in their (and our) inspired set of books! The book of Jonah makes God's prophet and His people look bad and Israel's worst enemy, Assyria, look good. Would Adventists, or any group, want to preserve and canonize a book that portrayed them in a bad light and pictured one of their worst enemies (atheists?) in a good light? Israel, under the prompting of God's Spirit, did just that when she put the book of Jonah in the Bible!

All of this was meant to jar Israel out of her self-centeredness and lead her to begin to reach out to other nations and be missionary minded. Israel was meant to be just like God with His great missionary heart. So are we, and that is the great lasting message of Jonah.

■ Getting Into the Word

Read Jonah through twice. During the second reading, look for details you might have missed earlier. As you read, note answers to the following questions:

1. **Imagine you are a Jew. You have been taught from birth to detest Assyria and its capital, Nineveh, as an enemy and to love and respect your own country, Israel. List all the things in the book of Jonah that would bother you. What happens in the book that would raise questions about the "truth" you had been taught?**
2. **Jonah's words and actions tell a lot about what he believes concerning God. As you read, make a list of Jonah's ideas about God. What parts of Jonah's "theology" do you agree with? What parts do you disagree with? Why?**

Jonah the Man

The book of Jonah is named after its chief character, who is portrayed as a prophet. The book does not specifically identify its author and speaks in the third person of Jonah, but tradition has ascribed authorship of the book to him.

Jonah means "dove." Hosea 7:11 portrays Ephraim, a synonym for the northern kingdom of Israel, as a dove that is "easily deceived and senseless." This means the name could actually be a symbol of the character of the man Jonah or even a nickname showing his personality. In English, we term people who are fearful "chicken." Jonah's name could be used in a similar way.

Jonah is the son of Ammitai. Nothing is known about Ammitai, but the name does give a sense of history to Jonah. According to 2 Kings 14:25, Jonah comes from Gath Hepher, which is in the territory of the tribe of Zebulon. The city was of moderate size and probably is to be identified with Khirbet ez-Zurra, three miles northeast of Nazareth (Stuart, 431). This is within the boundaries of the northern kingdom where Jonah prophesied concerning the re-expansion of the northern kingdom under Jeroboam II (793–753 B.C.). (See 2 Kings 14:23-27).

The book portrays Jonah as narrow, stubborn, and hypocritical, but a prophet nonetheless. If Jonah himself wrote the book, we would also have to see him as brutally honest and possessing a sense of humor. A special kind of person would be needed to tell such a story about oneself.

Historical Setting

The historical setting of the book is the early- to mid-eighth century B.C. (800–750 B.C.). Assyria is a major foreign power (probably *the* major foreign power) opposed to Israel. Nineveh is its capital. Jonah resides in the northern kingdom and works as a prophet, which includes prophecy about the growth of the northern kingdom under Jeroboam II (2 Kings 14:23-27). Suddenly Jonah is told to go to Assyria and prophesy in its capital city. The book is the story of Jonah's response to this command and God's action.

Because of the nature and uniqueness of Jonah's story, many questions have been raised about its historical setting. Is it true? Was the book written in the time of Jonah, or is it a much later composition?

Without going into great detail, I would like to suggest that the book does have a basis in history and was written at a time near to the portrayed historical setting. The story about Jonah's other prophesying in 2 Kings 14:25 should be taken seriously. The account in Kings mentions not only the name of Jonah, but also names his father Ammitai.

We seem to be dealing with the same Jonah (with the same father) at the right historical period.

The story of Jonah contains many similarities to the Elijah-Elisha narratives that also come from this period. These two prophets, like Jonah, had ministries in foreign countries (1 Kings 17:7-24; 2 Kings 8:7-17). Thus Jonah's foreign ministry is not entirely out of context.

Also of importance in understanding the historical background is the fact that a key to the story is the saving of Nineveh. This would not have been meaningful if the story was written after 612 B.C. when Nineveh was destroyed. It would also seem strange to write such a book after the fall of the northern kingdom and its capital Samaria to Assyria in 722-721 B.C. No prophetic book by a northern-kingdom author is written after this event.

In dealing with the historicity of the book of Jonah, some also point to events in Assyria itself. During the reign of Semiranis, queen regent, and her son Adad-Nerai III (810–782 B.C.), there was a major religious reform in Assyria. This reform exhibited some characteristics of monotheism and was similar to the Amarna reform period in Egypt (Watts, 77). Some have suggested that this ninth-century reform was the one brought on by the preaching of Jonah. (For further arguments about the historicity of the Assyrian response, see Stuart, 490-492).

Theme and Message

Jonah is the greatest missionary book of the Old Testament. The book clearly shows God as One who cares deeply about nations other than His special people, Israel. Although the book begins with a proclamation of judgment on Nineveh, it ends with grace and salvation for that great city.

The basis for mission lies in the heart of God. He is the One who calls and sends Jonah. Even when Jonah avoids the call, God persists in reaching out to Nineveh. When the people repent, God responds in graciousness and forgives them and cancels the prophesied destruction.

The problem brought to view in the book of Jonah is the reluctance and unfaithfulness of God's called missionary, Jonah. The narrow-mindedness of Jonah and his pro-Israel bias are so plain that it would be almost funny if the matter weren't serious. The irony of the gracious God who has such an ungracious prophet is clear.

Adding to the irony, and perhaps to the humor, is Jonah's huge success in terms of audience response to his preaching. This displeases, rather than delights, Jonah, and we are left with a vivid picture of the distorting power of narrowness and bias.

The clear appeal of the book is for people to revise their picture of God and the world. God's plan, mission, and love are extremely broad and call into question all human prejudice and preconceived ideas. The double question in 4:4 and 4:9 points to God's appeal in this book. "What right do you have to be angry?" He asks Jonah. God continues to ask His people that question today.

Outline of Jonah
God's Missionary Heart

I. Introduction (1:1, 2)
    A. The messenger identified (1:1)
    B. The mission and message stated (1:2)
II. The Human Missionary Flees (1:3–2:10)
    A. Jonah attempts to flee (1:3-17)
    B. Jonah prays for deliverance (2:1-10)
III. The Divine Missionary Persists (3:1–4:11)
    A. God sends Jonah a second time (3:1-10)
    B. God teaches Jonah about mission (4:1-11)

CHAPTER THIRTEEN

The Human Missionary Flees

Jonah 1, 2

The first two chapters of Jonah outline the results of Jonah's misguided attempt to run away from God and His missionary call. Commanded to go and preach to Nineveh, Jonah disobeys and heads in the opposite direction. Problems soon develop, and Jonah ends up in the belly of a big fish, praying for deliverance. The story concludes with God's action forcing the large fish to vomit Jonah up on dry ground.

Along the way we find out a lot about Jonah, about God, about unbelievers, and about prayer. Careful reading of the story will teach us much that our childhood memories of the Jonah story probably don't contain. As you read and study, try to hear the story as if you were hearing it for the first time.

■ Getting Into the Word

Jonah 1, 2

Read Jonah 1 and 2 carefully twice, and answer the following questions:

1. Three important places are mentioned in Jonah—Nineveh (1:2), Tarshish, and Joppa (vs. 3). To these could be added Jonah's home town of Gath Hepher. Using the maps in your Bible or a Bible atlas or Bible dictionary, find the location of these four places. What is important about each of these

four cities? Why are they crucial to the story? What does their location contribute to our understanding of the story? Is Tarshish the same city as the hometown of Saul/Paul in the New Testament (see Acts 9:11)?

2. Jonah's time on the ship reveals much about the beliefs, theology, and religious practice of the non-Israelite sailors. Make a list of the things you learn about the religion of the sailors from the story in Jonah 1. Are these people religious? Are they open to truth and other religions? What reasons can you give for your answers?

3. God is active in the first two chapters of Jonah. Make a list of the specific things God does in these two chapters. What do they tell us about God? Do most Christians today still believe that God does all these things? Why, or why not? Should we still believe God does these things?

4. Look carefully at Jonah's prayer in chapter 2. What specifically does Jonah ask for? What is Jonah's attitude during the prayer? Does he repent? What beliefs about God does the prayer illustrate? What can we learn about prayer itself from Jonah's prayer? Can we today pray this way? Why?

5. People have debated for years whether the book of Jonah is to be taken literally or whether it is just a parable to teach a lesson. On the basis of these first two chapters, how would you answer the question? Give answers based on the text, and give reasons for your answers.

■ Exploring the Word

God's Word to Jonah and Jonah's Response

Jonah (1:1) begins in exactly the same way as do many prophetic books. The expression "the word of the Lord came to . . ." is the conventional way of introducing divine communication and occurs over one hundred times in the Old Testament. Most often the phrase introduces a specific message the prophet is commanded to deliver. Sometimes, as in Jonah, the phrase precedes specific instructions to the prophet. The clear message is that what follows is not a human invention but a divine command.

God tells Jonah to "get up" and "go" preach to Nineveh (vs. 2). (Note that the NIV translation leaves out the first word of the Hebrew command.) God directs Jonah to preach to Nineveh because "its wickedness has come up before me" (vs. 2). This phrase is somewhat ambiguous. God gives no specific explanation as to the nature of this "wickedness." The Hebrew word used here can mean either "wickedness" or "calamity." At least one scholar believes the second meaning should be the preferred translation (McComiskey, 500, 551). During this period Assyria did have some national setbacks. If God was more concerned over Assyria's problems than her sins, that would help explain Jonah's flight and his later complaints about God's mercy (4:1-3). Jonah, as a patriotic Israelite, would find it easier to talk about Assyrian sins than Assyrian national calamities. Whatever the case, the command to go to Nineveh is clear even if the exact message to be proclaimed is not. In this case, that is what matters most—Jonah's obedience or disobedience to God's orders.

Jonah immediately proceeds to disobey God and run away from Him. The prophet heads to Tarshish by way of the Judean port city of Joppa (1:3). A survey of the geography will help us understand the story.

Nineveh and Tarshish were at the opposite ends of the commercial world of Jonah's time. Nineveh, in Assyria, lay north and east of Gath Hepher, about 500 miles overland. The exact location of Tarshish is uncertain, but it was probably located at the far western end of the Mediterranean Sea. Assuming that Jonah started from Gath Hepher, his home, Joppa was already the first step in his flight. Other coastal ports were twice as close to Gath Hepher, but Joppa was the port one would use if he were traveling in the direction away from Nineveh. This natural harbor on the Mediterranean Sea, near modern Tel-Aviv, suited Jonah's plans.

Nineveh, called "the great city" (1:2, 3:2), was located on the Tigris River. Today its ruins lie just opposite the city of Mosul in northern Iraq. The name itself is a form of the word "Ishtar," the most popular goddess in the metropolis during Jonah's day. During the tenth century (B.C.) and beginning again with the reign of Sennacherib (about 700 B.C.), it served as the capital of the Assyrian Empire. Nineveh fell to Babylon conquerors and was destroyed in 612 B.C.

We know from archaeological excavations that the city contained the palaces of Sennacherib and Asshur-Banipal (669–626 B.C.) (Watts, 76). This last ruler left a vast library of 20,000 clay tablets, which include Mesopotamian stories of creation and a flood. As well as the goddess Ishtar, the city venerated the corn god Dagon. We will examine the size and population of the city in the next chapter.

In the book of Jonah, Nineveh is symbolically bigger than a literal city. It stands for the world outside of Israel. In a real sense, those who are not part of the covenant are "Nineveh."

We do not know for sure the exact location of Tarshish. Several towns in the western Mediterranean area, including a place in Spain, were known as Tarshish or by a similar name. All of them were mining or smelting centers for silver, iron, tin, and lead (Watts, 77). They shipped their materials on the largest freighters of the day, which were called "ships of Tarshish." This place has nothing to do with Saul's hometown of Tarsus in the New Testament. That city lay at the opposite end of the Mediterranean Sea in Cilicia.

As Nineveh was, in a sense, symbolic, so is Tarshish. Tarshish is as far away from God's plan as one can get. Tarshish is any attempt to get out of the reach of God.

Heroes of the Story

The Gentile sailors on the ship Jonah boarded are in stark contrast to Jonah, the prophet of Yahweh, who flees from his God. When the storm strikes, the sailors each pray and cry out to their god (1:5). The captain himself seeks out Jonah and calls on him to likewise seek *his* God for deliverance (vs. 6). The sailors are terrified and appalled when they find out Jonah is running from God (vs. 10). Jonah asks to be thrown into the sea, but the sailors at first refuse and try to row to shore (vss. 12, 13). Failing in their attempt and realizing that they must do as Jonah suggests, the sailors pray to Yahweh (vs. 14), Israel's God, asking Him to forgive them for their act. With Jonah overboard, the sea becomes calm, and these sailors "fear" the Lord and offer sacrifices and vows to Him (vs. 16). The fourfold mention of Yahweh's name (twice each in verses 14 and 16) makes it clear the book is telling us that these men have come to acknowledge Yahweh, Israel's and Jonah's God, as worthy of faith and worship.

The contrast between God's prophet and these pagan sailors is amazing!

Jonah	**Foreign Sailors**
Fleeing from God	Running to God in prayer
Sleeping below deck	Working and praying on deck
Unconcerned about others	Trying to save others (Jonah)
Disobeyed God in face of much evidence	Believing and obeying God with little evidence

Through this powerful story, the smug, self-righteous attitude of Jonah and his Israelite compatriots is being systematically destroyed. The heathen Gentiles are more religious and ethical than God's own people. The targets of mission are more righteous than the missionary! The outsiders are more God-fearing than the insider.

When Jonah is thrown overboard, he is swallowed by a "great fish" that the Lord provides. This fish is the most well-known character in the book! Strange as it may seem, he/she/it is mentioned in only three verses—1:17 and 2:1, 10.

The word used in the text does not make it clear exactly what kind of fish this is. The term is the generic one for fish coupled with the adjective "large." We can more safely say what type of fish this is *not*. It is most likely not a whale, and it is certainly not the sinister sea serpent or monster in some places called "Leviathan" (Isaiah 27:1). The emphasis in the book of Jonah is on the gracious provision by God for the prophet's preservation in time of trouble. The fish is God's saving agent, not a symbol of evil.

In the book of Jonah, the real hero is clearly not Jonah or the sailors or the great fish. The main actor is God. The word *Lord* (from the Hebrew word for God's name—Yahweh) occurs twenty-five times. The word *God* appears thirteen times, and *Lord God* is used once. This makes a total of thirty-nine references to the Divine Being in the forty-four verses of the book. God is center stage. What exactly is He doing? It is instructive to make a list of God's specific acts just in these first two chapters.

1. He speaks to Jonah (1:1).
2. He sends a great wind (1:4).
3. He provides a fish to swallow Jonah (1:17).
4. He hears prayers (1:24; 2:2).
5. He causes the fish to vomit Jonah onto dry land (2:10).

The God of Jonah is obviously active not only in human lives, but in the realm of nature as well. Not only can He speak and listen to people, but He is master of storms and big fish.

A True Story?

One of the major problems people of the twentieth century have with the book of Jonah is this portrayal of a God who acts so directly. They question such specific action. Some can accept a God who hears and answers prayer but wonder about a God who can command nature so directly. Others doubt all such activities of God, while many see no problem at all in believing that God does all these things.

I, myself, struggle with this issue. Being raised, socialized, and educated in the skeptical world of the west, I must admit I have some questions about a man-swallowing fish. Living for years as a missionary in Asia has helped me be much more open to the direct action of God. I certainly believe God *can* literally do everything portrayed in the book of Jonah.

My biggest problem is knowing how to talk to people about this issue and how to teach the book of Jonah. Some will dismiss the story of Jonah if they think they must take every act of God in the book literally. That grieves me, because Jonah's basic message is not about this issue. The message of the book concerns the gracious, loving, missionary heart of God contrasted with the narrowness of God's people.

On the other hand, there are those whose faith in the book would be shaken if someone claimed Jonah was not actually swallowed by a divinely-provided, literal fish. In other words, if everything is *not* literal, they would want to discard this book and maybe the whole Bible. The tragedy is that *both* groups miss the real lesson God is trying to teach in this book. Both sides stumble over the wrappings and never find what is inside the package.

I would like to suggest that both sides attempt to temporarily hold in suspension the issue of the reality of God's direct action as it relates to the question of whether the whole book (or parts) is literal or symbolic. Both groups must recognize that the book of Jonah assumes that its readers believe in God's direct action in human lives and in nature. Jonah would be appalled to find that there are people who miss his message because they quarrel over this issue. Jonah wants to tell us to abandon bigotry, narrowness, ethnocentrism, and national pride. He wants to urge us to build an openness to others that leads to mission. To miss that message would be a tragedy. Listen and accept this truth before you go on to debate how God acts.

Don't misunderstand me! As I said earlier, I personally believe God can do all these things. I don't want that belief, however, to keep some from really hearing the basic missionary message Jonah cares most about giving. The lesson of Jonah does not depend on the literalness of God's causing a fish to vomit a prophet onto dry ground!

Once we recognize that point, we can go on to discuss the question of literalness. I believe that certain aspects of the text point to a literal reading of the book. Note the following:

1. The main character in the book is presented as a historical person. Jonah and his father are named, and as mentioned earlier, the historical book of 2 Kings (14:25) mentions a man named Jonah who appears to be the same person in a similar historical setting.

2. The introduction of the book mirrors other sections and books

of the Bible that are historical. An example would be 1 Kings 17:8, 9, "The word of the Lord came to him [Elijah], 'Arise, go to Zarephath' " (RSV). Anyone familiar with Hebrew narrative would expect such an introduction to be treated as the beginning of a factual narrative (Alexander et al).

3. The first two chapters read like an historical account. Real place names are mentioned. People interact in a believable, factual way. Although God's action is spoken of, it is not unduly emphasized or elaborated.

We should remember, too, that attempts to read the book other than as a factual account are of relatively recent origin. Most efforts to make the book symbolic stem from a worldview that has difficulty with the direct action of God in human life. That worldview is culturally related and conditioned just as is the opposing belief that God can act directly in human life and in nature.

Jonah's Prayer

Jonah's second chapter is a change of pace. What has been a story in prose becomes a prayer in poetry. What has been a fleeing sinner becomes a seeking penitent. Before we heard pagan sailors in prayer, now we hear the reluctant missionary calling out to God.

Jonah's prayer from the belly of the fish has often been misunderstood. The prayer does *not* concern Jonah's experience inside the fish but what happened to him in the sea *before* the fish swallowed him. Jonah's distress is not over his experience in the fish but over his near-drowning episode before the fish arrived. Note that the main verbs in the passage are *past* tense: "I called . . . and you listened (2:2), "You hurled me" (vs. 3), "I said" (vs. 4), etc. Jonah from within the belly of the big fish is meditating on the recent past.

The "psalm" of Jonah does not seem to have a time progression. Actually, it reflects on his almost-drowning experience in four cycles: (1) verse 2; (2) verses 3, 4; (3) verses 5, 6; and (4) verse 7. In each of these stanzas, or cycles, there is a reference to death and a particular problem that Jonah experienced.

Reference to Death	Problem
1. Depths of the grave (Sheol, RSV) (vs. 2)	Distress (vs. 2)
2. Banished from God's sight (vs. 4)	Currents, waves, breakers (vs. 3)
3. The pit (vs. 6)	Waters trapped in earth beneath (vss. 6, 7)
4. Life ebbing away (vs. 7)	Life ebbing away (vs. 7)

Repeated reference is also made to Jonah's praying (2:1, 2, 7), using both the terms *pray* and *call*. According to Jonah, God "answered" and "listened" (vs. 2). God's answer, of course, was the fish. Jonah had thought he would die of drowning and in desperation calls out to God. In spite of Jonah's disobedience and rebellion, God answers him and saves him in a divinely-provided, fishy submarine!

This leads Jonah to respond in two ways. First, he recalls how worthless idols are and how helpless and unable to help they seem to be (vs. 8). Second, in contrast he will praise God and perform sacrifices and vows to recognize God's wonderful salvation (vs. 9).

Ironically, the Gentile sailors have not only been praying and urging others to pray (1:5, 6), but have already offered sacrifices and vows to Yahweh (vs. 16). For Jonah, the supposed pious Israelite, it has taken a near-death encounter and a miraculous deliverance to bring him to prayer and religious vows.

Jonah's entire experience in fleeing from God has been *down*. Down to Joppa (vs. 3) and then down below deck on the ship (vs 5). The sailors threw him down into the sea (vs 15). In Jonah 2 he goes down to the "depths of the grave" (vs. 2) and into the "deep" (vs. 3). The deep surrounds him (vs. 5), and he descends to the very "roots of the mountains" (vs. 6), which was as far down as one could go. From these very depths, however, God brings him up (vs. 6) and delivers him. All the "downs" are turned by God into a great "up."

Clearly, a disobedient Jonah does not deserve to be saved in answer to prayer. Only God's mercy can do such things—not justice. This experience lays a basis for what happens in chapter 4. How ironic that a rebellious Jonah should receive grace and mercy in response to a desperate prayer and then be angry when God is equally gracious to a rebellious Nineveh. He manifests an all-too-common human characteristic—to joyously receive mercy for one's own self but respond angrily if a loving God manifests the same mercy to someone else, especially an enemy.

Jonah's prayer, and chapter 2, conclude with a brief comment that God commands the fish, and it deposits Jonah on dry land. Jonah has said nothing in his prayer about his missionary call. No reprimand has been verbalized. God has simply brought Jonah back to where he started.

If you had never read the rest of the book or knew the rest of the story, this would be a great place to pause, reflect, and ask some questions. What will happen now? What will God do? Will He pick another prophet/missionary? Will He tell Jonah to repent? What has Jonah learned? How does he feel? What will happen to Nineveh? Stay tuned as we study the powerful conclusion to this book in the next chapter.

■ Applying the Word

Jonah 1, 2

1. **Do you know anyone who has tried to run away from God? Have you? What do you think happens when people try to escape God? Can running away from God be something not necessarily geographical? Can we try to run away by getting busy or trying to drown out God's voice? In what ways?**

2. **Do you know non-Christian people who are more religious than some supposed believers you are acquainted with? Describe them. What would it take for them to make sacrifices and vows to Yahweh? What can such people teach us?**

3. **Where and/or what is Tarshish for you? Where and/or what is Nineveh for you? Joppa? What are the places you should go and don't want to? Where do you want to go that you shouldn't go? How have God and other people helped to bring you back where you should be?**

4. **What do Jonah's prayer and God's answer teach us about**

prayer? Does God hear and answer desperate prayers? Always? Sometimes? Why did God answer Jonah's? Why does the Bible record Jonah's prayer *after* the deliverance rather than his prayer *for* deliverance?

5. Who are your enemies? Whom do you dislike? Who do you think is far from God? Why do you feel this way? What are the reasons? Are they valid? What if God called you to go speak to such people? How would you respond?

■ Researching the Word

1. Many scholars compare Jonah to Elijah and Elisha and their ministries. You can review the stories of these two prophets by beginning in 1 Kings 17 and continuing on into the book of 2 Kings. Is this a valid comparison? How is Jonah's experience similar to those of Elijah and Elisha? If they are similar, what does this tell us about the book of Jonah?

2. The phrase "three days and three nights" (1:17), used to describe Jonah's stay in the fish's belly, also appears in other places in Scripture, such as Matthew 12:40, Mark 16:4, and Luke 11:29-32. What does the phrase really mean? Use a concordance to find all the places in which this phrase is used. Why is it used here in Jonah? What does this teach us about the way the Bible counted time? You may also want to examine the treatment of the Gospel's use of this phrase in the *Seventh-day Adventist Bible Commentary* or in some other commentary.

■ Further Study of the Word

1. For a general background to Jonah 1, 2, see Ellen G. White, *Prophets and Kings*, 265-269.

2. For an in-depth defense of a literal historical view of Jonah, see Hubbard, *Themes From the Minor Prophets*, 66-77.

3. For a general introduction to the interpretation of Jonah, see LaSor, et al., *Old Testament Survey*, 347-355.

CHAPTER FOURTEEN

The Divine Missionary Persists

Jonah 3, 4

God's call does come a second time to Jonah. No condemnation or appeal for repentance is made. Yahweh simply commands once more that Jonah go to Nineveh and preach. Finally the human missionary responds to the persistent call of the Divine Missionary. That, however, is not the solution to all of Jonah's or Nineveh's or even God's problems.

The body of Jonah changes direction, but his mind and heart remain the same. These last two chapters of the book outline Yahweh's work to alter Jonah's bigoted, ungracious heart and turn it into a heart of love and mercy—a missionary heart. Amazingly, in spite of the human missionary's sin and failing, the mission to change Nineveh has stupendous success. Nineveh's king and people repent and turn to God. This success does not end the story; God does not give up on His mission to change the heart of the missionary. God wants not only to save Nineveh, but His prophet as well.

■ Getting Into the Word

Jonah 3, 4

Read Jonah 3 and 4 carefully twice, and then answer the following questions:

1. These two chapters reveal many things about Nineveh—size, population, government, people's understanding, and even livestock. List all the facts about Nineveh you can glean

from these chapters. If you want to find out more, consult a Bible dictionary or encyclopedia under the word *Nineveh*.

2. In this section, God makes a time prophecy to Nineveh. What is this prophecy, and what is the time period involved? This prophecy does not reach fulfillment. Why? What does this teach us about God and conditional prophecy? Was there any mention of conditionality when the prophecy was given? How should this story affect the way we understand prophecy? In what ways does Jeremiah 18:7-10 help us understand prophecy in the book of Jonah?

3. Contrast Nineveh's response to God and Jonah's preaching with Jonah's response to Nineveh's deliverance. What seems to be the attitude of each party? What are the reasons for these attitudes? What is the book of Jonah trying to teach us by telling us about this contrast?

4. Analyze Jonah's angry prayer (4:1-3). What are the main points of the prayer? Why exactly was Jonah angry? Should Jonah have prayed in this situation? Why? What is God's response to the prayer? What does this passage teach us about prayer? How does all of this fit with Jonah's prayer in the belly of the fish in chapter 2?

5. In Jonah 4:6-8 the phrase, "God provided," is used three times. What does God provide each time? What are the purposes of each provision God makes? What does this tell us about the kinds of things God provides for us?

6. The book ends with a question and sounds almost unfinished. What is the question, and why was it asked? What is the question supposed to do? Is this a good way to end the book? Why?

■ Exploring the Word

Nineveh Receives the Message

God proves Himself to be a giver of second chances. His missionary heart persists in calling men and women to Himself. No time element is mentioned, but probably soon after God's great fish de-

posits Jonah on dry land, the word of the Lord comes to Jonah the
second time (3:1). The command God gives is twofold: (a) "Go to
the great city of Nineveh" (vs. 2). I like the vividness of the original
Hebrew which says literally, "Rise! [Get up!] Go!" (b) "Proclaim to
it the message I give you" (vs. 2). Jonah is not to speak his own words
but specifically the words Yahweh gives to him.

In contrast to his initial response, which was flight, this time Jonah
obeys and goes to Nineveh (vs. 2). We will soon find out that although
Jonah has, in body, gone as a missionary to Nineveh, his feelings about
Nineveh have *not* changed. His body and mouth are missionary, but his
heart and mind are still runaways. Nevertheless, Jonah's missionary experience will become God's way of changing his heart.

What is this city Nineveh like? What kind of place was it that
God wanted warned and saved?

1. The city was important. Three times in Jonah 3 and 4 the city is
specifically called great or important (3:2, 3; 4:11). The second such
reference in 3:3 is interesting because it says literally in Hebrew that
Nineveh was "great to God." Stuart rightly translates the phrase,
"Nineveh was a city important to God" (Stuart, 483). Some have
seen these statement about greatness as particularly relating to size.
Nineveh was quite large by ancient standards, but I believe the "greatness" of Nineveh was more than just size. Nineveh was a key part of
God's plan and mattered to Him and to the ancient world.

Jonah 3:3 says that Nineveh was "three days' journey in breadth"
(RSV) or "a visit required three days" (NIV). What does this mean?
The phrase "three days" has been a question in many people's minds.

The traditional interpretation has been to relate this statement to
size. However, since archaeological excavations have revealed that the
later imperial city of Nineveh was about eight miles in circumference
the reference has raised questions. The phrase could refer to the size of
the larger Nineveh area, which was composed of Nineveh and four
satellite cities—Rehoboth, Ir, Calah, and Resen, mentioned in Genesis
10:11, 12 (Barker, 1368). This area was about sixty miles in circumference and would fit this three-day statement if it refers to size.

Another possible meaning for this phrase has been suggested by
D. J. Wiseman (Wiseman, 29-51). The issue here may be "the an-

cient oriental practice of hospitality whereby the first day is for arrival, the second for the primary purpose of the visit, and the third
for return" (Wiseman, 38). This would mean that Jonah was sent as
an official emissary and was received by officials and people alike.
The point is that Nineveh was a major diplomatic center. Formal
protocol was observed, and business could not be accomplished hastily as it might be in an insignificant, small town. This would also
help explain the reason for Jonah's speedy success.

Jonah 4:11 portrays the city of Nineveh as having a population of
at least 120,000 people. While some have suggested that this 120,000
represents only the children of Nineveh since they are the ones who
don't know their right hand from their left, this is probably not so. I
suggest that it represents the total population of Nineveh or the
greater Nineveh four-city complex. All the city was ignorant of
God—not just children. For ancient cities, 120,000 people would
still be a very populous metropolis.

In sum, Nineveh was not only "great" in size and population, but
also great in importance—to both God and the ancient world.

2. Nineveh was needy. Nineveh was about to be "overturned" in
judgment because of her sins (1:2; 3:4). She needed desperately to
be warned, and God worked hard to make sure Jonah did this.

Ninevites were also, as mentioned above, people who did not know
their right hand from their left (4:11). This idiomatic expression
means a lack of knowledge or innocence (Stuart, 507). Perhaps the
phrase could also mean "helpless" or "pitiful." This phrase applies
to the whole population of Nineveh, not just to children.

This does not signify that the Ninevites were innocent of moral
wrong. Otherwise, why would God see it as fair or right to judge
them as He did? Rather, they were innocent in the sense they did
not know how to escape from where they found themselves. Caught
in a cultural social web of polytheism, idolatry, and moral evil, they
did not know how to break free. Only God's divine message and
messenger could give them an avenue of escape. Nineveh was needy
because she saw no way out of her dilemma. She was to be pitied.

3. Nineveh was responsive. Jonah 3 portrays the most numerically successful preaching series in the Bible. Jonah 3:5 says simply "the Ninevites

believed God." They fasted, put on sackcloth and sat in the dust—all signs of mourning and repentance from their sins. This, according to Scripture, was done by "all of them, from the greatest to the least" (vs. 5). This includes the king, who issued a proclamation (vss. 6-9), and the livestock as well as everything in between. The fact that animals are mentioned points out the corporate nature of the way Ninevites viewed life and the comprehensiveness of the situation. Everybody, and all they were and had, responded to the message.

The king's decree in verses 7-9 is particularly instructive. Not only are the people and livestock to fast and be covered with sackcloth, they are to call on God and pray urgently. They are to renounce their evil ways in hopes that they will be saved, although that is in no way sure. This decree shows a very profound and mature response. Nothing is superficial about his repentance.

Some have questioned the historicity of such a dramatic sweeping response to Jonah's preaching. They see the account as an obvious exaggeration lacking in historical reliability. In response, I must say this is not necessarily so. The study of ancient Assyrian religious texts teaches us that there are at least four circumstances when such a response from a king and people would be called for: (1) invasion by an enemy, (2) total solar eclipse, (3) famine joined with epidemic, and (4) a severe flood (Stuart, 490). If Jonah, in God's timing, had arrived during or immediately following one of these four events in Nineveh, the reaction outlined in the book of Jonah could easily have taken place. The Assyrian belief system itself would have laid the groundwork for the reception of Jonah's message.

We should also notice that the message of the book of Jonah does not depend on this tremendous response for its impact. A much less dramatic and/or smaller response could also have resulted in the cancellation of God's judgment. The persistence of God in leading Jonah to Nineveh may have related to this timing as well. God knew about the receptivity of Nineveh and made sure His prophet arrived at the most propitious time.

After this wonderful response, the great question now is, What will God do? How will He respond to the repentance of Nineveh and her plea for mercy?

Yahweh Responds

Recall that Yahweh has not simply given a judgment prophecy to Nineveh through Jonah. It was a *timed* judgment prophecy. "Forty more days and Nineveh will be overturned (3:4). No "ifs" or conditions were stated. No "maybes" were attached. A time was set in straightforward fashion.

When Nineveh repented, God responded. "When God saw what they did and how they turned from their evil ways, He had compassion and did *not* bring upon them the destruction He had threatened" (Jon. 3:10, emphasis supplied). God did *not* fulfill His own prophecy. This experience teaches us profound lessons about the nature of prophecy. We can begin to learn these lessons by noting the two reasons given for Yahweh's change of mind in Jonah 3:10:

1. The repentance of the people. God saw and knew what they did in response to the preaching, and this was part of His basis for action.

2. God's compassion. God cared and loved so much that He saved the people. People and compassion take precedence over a prophecy, timing, and a formal kind of consistency. Prophecy is not some rigid, timeless statement that governs history, irrespective of human response. Prophecy is affected by people and their actions and by the heart of God, which takes into account all aspects of life. Even though no conditional factor is stated, it seems to be assumed by both God and the Ninevites, and rightly so.

Jeremiah 18:7-10 is the classic statement on conditional prophecy, and Jonah is a prime example of its principles. "If at any time I announce that a nation or kingdom is to be uprooted, torn down and destroyed, and if that nation I warned repents of its evil, then I will relent and not inflict on it the disaster I had planned" (Jer. 18: 7, 8). According to Jeremiah, the opposite is also true. If God prophesies good for a nation and it sins, God will reconsider the good He intended for it.

Prophecy, then, is always related to a specific historical situation and based on God's present analysis of it. When that situation changes, the evaluation and analysis of it change. The proclamation of prophecy is not an announcement of an unchangeable decree that seals one's doom, but a heartfelt appeal to change the situation so God's compassion can be shown. If you are interested in digging deeper into this issue, note the first question in the Researching the Word section at the end of this chapter.

Jonah's Response

We have examined Nineveh and her response to God's appeal. We've also explored God's mercy to Nineveh and the altering of His sentence of judgment. What about God's human missionary? How did Jonah relate to all this? While Jonah 3 emphasizes how Nineveh responded to the message of Jonah, Jonah 4 spotlights the prophet's response to Nineveh's and God's actions.

Jonah's response is divided into two parts. First, 4:1-4 see Jonah pouring out his anger and frustration to God in prayer (4:1-3). God's response comes in the form of a question (vs. 4). Second, Jonah 4:5-11 relates the story of the gourd plant and the worm and exposes Jonah's faulty thinking while revealing, in contrast, the caring concern of Yahweh.

The time frame of these two sections is not certain. One way of looking at it is to see the first section (4:1-4) as Jonah's response when he finds out about God's decision to not punish Nineveh. The last section (vss. 5-11) is a flashback to an earlier time when the outcome was still unknown and Jonah had some hope that Nineveh would be destroyed. This last section concludes the book, revealing the compassionate heart of God in contrast to the narrow hardness of Jonah's heart.

Another view is to see the two sections as both taking place after Jonah hears about God's decision. They follow in chronological order. Jonah vents his anger about God's decision and asks for the Lord to destroy him. This is a request for God to reconsider His decision and abide by His promise of destruction. In the second part (vss. 5-11), Jonah sits down to see if God will answer his plea and destroy the city. The Lord's reply to Jonah gives the reason why God cannot answer that request and cater to the narrowmindedness of His missionary.

Whichever of these two scenarios is true, the basic message is clear. Jonah deeply resents God's mercy and desperately desires the

destruction of Nineveh. He is so angry he would rather die than see
Nineveh saved.

Notice the contrasts between Jonah and the Ninevites.

	Nineveh	Jonah
Feeling/Emotion	Sorrow for sin	Anger over others' salvation
Action	Mourning practices, fast	Waiting for destruction of another
Prayer	For mercy	For recrimination
Desire	Hope for life	Hope for death
Divine Response	Compassion	Teaching, admonition
Motive	Saving of self and others	Protection of reputation

The good news for angry Jonah is that God has mercy on *him*. Jonah
4 is the story of how God's final mission in Jonah is doing that which is
the hardest mission of all—changing the heart of His missionary. How
God does that is the subject of our next section. There we will examine
that issue in detail. You will notice that I take the two sections to be in
chronological order, following the option I have explained above. This
seems to me to be the best way to read the story.

God's Three Questions

God's training class for Jonah centers around three questions that
God asks Jonah (4:4, 9, 11). These three questions are meant to
teach Jonah (and us) where his thinking has gone wrong and how
God views the situation. Although the book ends in a question, there
is no doubt what the implied answer to the question should be.

Question number one occurs at the end of Jonah's prayer (vss. 2-
4). The prayer is occasioned by Jonah's intense anger over God's
decision not to punish Nineveh. In a fit of rage and accompanying
depression, Jonah cries out to God. Jonah's prayer reveals the reason for his earlier flight toward Tarshish. He was afraid that God in

His mercy would *not* destroy Nineveh, and he wants no part in the deliverance of Nineveh.

Jonah's belief in God's compassion goes back to basic Israelite theology originally found in Exodus 34: 6, 7 and repeated with slight variation in Numbers 14:18, Psalm 86:15, 103:8, 145:8, Nahum 1:3, and Nehemiah 9:17. These passages talk about all the attributes of God mentioned in Jonah 4:2 except the last one, which says God "relents from sending calamity." That phrase also appears in Joel 2:13 and is illustrated in Amos 7:1-6. That statement is particularly relevant, of course, to what has happened in this story about Jonah and Nineveh.

What does all of this mean? Clearly, a theology which sees God as compassionate, gracious, and long-suffering is deeply embedded in Israel's mind. That theology includes the belief that God changes His course of action when people change. Call it "turning," "repenting," "relenting," or some other word, but God does it and does it regularly. Jonah was so convinced of this theology that he was willing to try to run away from God rather than see God act this way in relationship to Nineveh. This theology was thus not just an intellectual doctrine, but a theology that governed life and action and was part of Jonah's (and Israel's) very being. Seeing this theology in action on behalf of Nineveh is so disgusting to Jonah that he wants to die (vs. 3). Personally and professionally (as a prophet of his people Israel) he cannot face the implication of having a part in saving Israel's enemy Assyria.

Into this situation Yahweh inserts His first teaching question: "Have you any right to be angry?" (vs. 4). God gives no condemnation or scolding. He does not respond to Jonah's foolish request to die. No defensiveness is manifested. Just a simple question to awaken reason in the mind of Jonah. God is saying, "Think about it, Jonah! Do you have any right to be this way?"

Clearly, the implied answer is No. Jonah has no right to be angry. In particular, his own recent experience illustrates this. In mercy God has saved him from drowning. He should have perished in the sea because of his sins. Not only that, God's call to him has come a second time. God has just recently worked two compassionate, merciful deliverances in Jonah's own life. What right does he have to get mad when God shows mercy to someone else?

I believe Jonah began to think about things at this point but still was not really changed. He still felt he was more righteous and deserving than Nineveh. He also was God's prophet and may have felt that in mercy to him God would hear his desperate prayer and change His mind again and destroy Nineveh. Because he hoped such a thing would happen, Jonah exited Nineveh toward the east and sat down to watch and wait (vs. 5). After all, God has said forty days and Nineveh would be destroyed. If there was any chance that might still happen, Jonah wanted to be sure and see it. In that situation God continued His work with Jonah.

God proceeds to "provide" three things to teach Jonah. Jonah has made himself a rough shelter outside the city. The word used to describe his shelter is the same word used for the temporary booths Jews built during the feast of booths (tabernacles). God provided a quick-growing gourd vine to grow up the rough walls and over the roof of the shelter and help shade Jonah (vs. 6). The vine eases Jonah's discomfort from the heat of the sun and makes Jonah very happy.

God then provides a worm (vs. 7) that kills the vine, and it withers. Third, God provides a scorching east wind to accompany the blazing sun (vs. 8). Jonah grew faint and wanted again to die. A long tradition exists in the Middle East that says the scorching scirocco winds cause bizarre behavior. In some Muslim countries, the penalty for crimes committed during the scirocco may be reduced because of the effect the winds have on thinking and acting (Stuart, 505, 506).

In response to Jonah's statement about desiring to die, God poses His second teaching question: "Do you have a right to be angry about the vine?" This second question is really a more direct application of the first question. The occurrence and the question are so close together, how can Jonah miss the point? But he does! He misses God's implied answer of No. He says in effect, "Yes, I do, and I'm angry enough to die" (vs. 9b).

God does not stop there, but continues the dialogue, which leads up to question three. God points out that Jonah is concerned about the vine that he had nothing to do with. He did not tend it or make it grow. It was given and then taken away. In contrast with one plant, Nineveh has more than 120,000 people who are helplessly trapped, as well as much livestock. Are not 120,000 people and much livestock more important than one plant (vs. 11)? With the third question, the point is clearly driven home. The comparison is appropriate, and the conclusion is not debatable. Even if there were no *people*, much livestock is more important than one plant!

Chapter 4 and God's three questions are specifically designed to lead Jonah and Israel to see the pettiness, narrowness, and logical inconsistency of their position. To receive God's mercy themselves and then begrudge God's gift of grace to those who were not Jews is not only illogical, but wrong. God cannot tolerate that attitude because it is contrary to His character. Jonah's and Israel's minds must change.

Conclusion

The very order of these last two chapters of Jonah is very instructive to us. A typical evangelical would have thought that chapter 3 would be the end of the story. After all, the evangelistic series in Nineveh had been overwhelmingly successful. Thousands had been saved and brought into God's family. Isn't that what missionary work is? Shouldn't that complete the story?

But chapter 4 of Jonah carries on. From God's viewpoint, missionary work is not completed when the heathen are converted and gathered in. The missionary God is concerned about something else. He wants to see if the *missionary* has been really converted.

Evangelistic success in Jonah is *not* related directly to spiritual growth, personal holiness, and correct theology. Jonah has phenomenal missionary success while he is a bigoted, angry, prejudiced, Jewish redneck. Evangelistic success does not signify theological correctness. God often does miraculous things through flawed instruments.

As in Jonah's case, true conversion of the missionary may come after successful completion of the conversion of the heathen. This evangelic success can be used by God to alter the attitude of the missionary and make it broader and more compassionate. Only then is the mission of the missionary God complete. I suspect that many of us have a part of Jonah residing in us. Either we don't want to go, or we go but our attitudes show we are still victims of Jonah-like thoughts. The Missionary God desires to use the book of Jonah to change us on both counts!

■ Applying the Word

Jonah 3, 4

1. Do you know God as the God who gives second (or third or fourth) chances? When in your life has God given you another chance? Do you give other people a second chance? What lies behind giving or receiving another chance?

2. For Christians today, what would be Nineveh? To what populous, sinful, important places are we hesitant to go? Cities? The Muslim, Buddhist, or Hindu world? AIDS victims? Who are our important enemies? Are there people today who are trapped and don't know their right hand from their left? Who?

3. Is the fact that God changes or relents, good news or bad news to you? Why? In the story, it was actually good news to both Nineveh and Jonah, but the latter didn't realize it. Why? If the fact that God changes is bad news to us, what does it say about our beliefs and attitudes?

4. Be honest. Have you ever gotten angry at God for something He did or did not do? What was it? Why did you get angry? Were you willing to express your anger? If so, how? Notice how God was able to teach Jonah when he expressed his anger. Hidden anger is harder to deal with. Why? What are proper ways to express anger? What do these passages teach us about anger in our life?

5. God uses three questions in Jonah 4 to teach His stubborn prophet. Why do you think He does so? What can questions do that straightforward statements may not do? Do you know someone who teaches by questions? How do they do it? How can we use questions effectively in our teaching of others?

6. What is your shading vine? What gives you comfort and shelter and makes you happy but really doesn't have much eternal value? What would you be upset about if it were taken away from you? What would you complain to God about if it were taken away? What do you think God would say to you about this?

■ Researching the Word

1. The issue of conditional prophecy is a vital one. Study, along with Jonah, the passage in Jeremiah 18. Look at the whole chapter in Jeremiah, and try to understand in that historical situation why the statement in 18:7-9 is made. Besides Jonah, Jeremiah 18, and Amos 7:1-6, can you find other instances of conditional prophecy in the Bible? What are they? What do all these passages teach us about our use of prophecy? Consider also this statement, "The promises and threatenings of God are alike conditional" (E.G. White, *Selected Messages*, 1:67). What does this mean in context? For more information, see Nichol, 4:34.

2. In Jonah 3, the people of Nineveh are mentioned as doing three specific actions in connection with their repentance: fasting, putting on sackcloth, and sitting in the dust (vss. 5-8). Use a concordance to find other Bible instances of such behavior. What besides repentance are these practices used for? What exactly does each of the three mean? Compare your findings with the discussion in a Bible dictionary.

3. Jonah 4 speaks repeatedly of Jonah's anger, while 3:9 mentions *God's* anger. Using a concordance, find other Bible references where prophets or priests express anger either in word or action. Note God's response to these shows of anger. What does this teach us about anger and its expressions?

■ Further Study of the Word

1. For general background to Jonah 3 and 4, see E. G. White, *Prophets and Kings*, 270-278.

2. For a discussion of Nineveh in relationship to the book of Jonah, see Alexander, et al., *Obadiah, Jonah, Micah*, 56-61.

3. For a delightful modern updating of the story of Jonah, see Corbett, *Prophets on Main Street*, 100-119.

4. For more insight into the graciousness of God, see Dybdahl, *Old Testament Grace*, 83-87.

PART SIX

Micah

Gloom
Yet
Greater Glory

CHAPTER FIFTEEN

Introduction to Micah

Micah is certainly one of the lesser known prophets. Even prophetic books of similar size, such as Amos, Joel, and Jonah, seem to be more famous. Part of the reason is that these three divine spokesmen have interesting personal stories in their books, which add human interest. Micah lacks such tales. In particular, Micah seems to live in the large shadow of his famous contemporary, Isaiah. I believe this obscurity is unjustified. Micah has an important message that deserves to be heard and that will richly reward the believer who takes the time to listen carefully to what he says.

Micah's book is unique in the way it is structured. The typical prophetic book follows a certain overall pattern made up of two major parts. Part one is doom or judgment. Often the doom is divided into two sections—a specific doom on God's people and a general judgment or doom on surrounding nations. The second major part of the pattern is hope—hope that God will restore what has been lost in judgment. Typically, the doom section is longer than the hope section. Micah deviates from this usual pattern in that while most prophetic books go through only one doom-to-hope cycle, Micah repeats the cycle three times in his book. These three cycles are found in 1:2–2:13; 3:1–5:15; and 6:1–7:20. Each of the three sections begin with the word hear *or* listen *(1:2; 3:1; 6:1), and each of their hope sections contain the motif of shepherding (2:12; 4:8; 5:4; 7:14) (see Alexander, et al., 145). This pattern ties the book together in a unity that may not be apparent at first.*

■ Getting Into the Word

Read the seven short chapters of Micah through carefully twice. As you read, look for answers to the following questions:

1. What can you find out about the person Micah from his book? The only information given directly in the text is that he is "of Moresheth" (1:1). Careful reading of a literary work, however, can tell us much about a person. From his book, see if you can determine whether Micah is from an urban or a rural background. Is he always stern, or does he also possess a sense of humor? Is he interested in nature or politics or geography? Is he unfeeling or sensitive to people and their emotions? What does he say that tells you these things? From his book, what makes you want—or not want—to know him personally?

2. The brief introduction to the book of Micah found above suggests that it is organized in a certain way. As you read, check to see if this suggested organization is really there. Do you find evidence for it? What is the evidence? Why do you think Micah organized his book this way? What advantage might it have over the typical prophetic book pattern?

Micah the Man

The direct material about the man Micah is scant. We have his name, *Micah*, probably a shortened form of Micaiah, which means "who is like Yahweh." He is not, however, to be equated with Micaiah, the son of Imlah, who was a prophet in the northern kingdom at the time of Ahab, ca 874–52 B.C. Micah in a very clever way inserts his name into the final hope section of his book. Using a play on his name, Micah asks in 7:18, "Who is a God like you . . ." in His wonderful capacity to pardon sin and forgive the transgression of His people. The implied answer is "No one!" Yahweh delights to show mercy and demonstrate compassion (vss. 1b, 19). His name, then, becomes symbolic for the restoration. God desires to give hope to

His people and shows Micah's message to be centered in the graciousness of Yahweh.

The only other specific fact about Micah given in his book is the naming of Moresheth as his hometown (1:1). Moresheth is most likely Moresheth Gath, which is located southwest of Jerusalem about halfway between the capital and the Mediterranean Sea. Although only about twenty miles from Jerusalem, the area is rural. Micah is thus a village or farm dweller in contrast to his urban, Jerusalem-dwelling contemporary, Isaiah.

Micah was linguistically gifted. The language he uses is vigorous and colorful. He utilizes many literary features and frequently resorts to figures of speech and puns that not only point to his cleverness, but suggest a sense of humor as well.

Historical Setting

Micah's introduction (1:1) tells us that he prophesied under three Judahite kings—Jotham, Ahaz, and Hezekiah. Although the prophet does comment on the northern kingdom of Israel, this statement shows that Micah clearly sees himself as a Judahite. His book demonstrates a deeply sensitive understanding of the social ills of his day, particularly as they relate to the southern kingdom.

Jotham (750–735 B.C.), Ahaz (735–715), and Hezekiah (715–686), although of the same dynasty, had very different characteristics. Jotham, according to 2 Kings (15:34, 35), did what was right in the sight of the Lord, even though his people still sacrificed and burned incense in the high places. Ahaz, his son and successor, was one of the most evil of Judahite kings. He even sacrificed his own children in the fire (2 Chron. 28:3) and did not shrink from putting an idol into the temple precincts itself (2 Kings 16:10-12, 14-17). Hezekiah, son of Ahaz, did all he could to reverse the religious evil endorsed by his father. He earned the praise of the writer of 2 Kings (18:5), "There was no one like him among all the kings of Judah, either before him or after him." The bulk of the material in Micah seems to relate to the period of the first two of these three kings.

The dominant foreign power during the period of Micah was

Assyria. Both Judah and Israel, as well as their neighbors, were heavily influenced by what Assyria did. Most nations at that time had conscripted citizen armies, but Assyria had a large full-time professional army, which none could match. As conquests were made, mercenaries were hired on as soldiers as well. Supported by heavy tributes exacted from subjugated territories, this professional army was free to enforce Assyrian rule and make new conquests.

Three significant events took place during the era of Micah that were related to Assyria (see Barker, 1370):

1. In 734-732 B.C. Tiglath Pileser III led a campaign against parts of Israel and Judah, as well as Syria and the land of the Philistines. Assyria won a resounding victory. All the nations had to pay tribute, but the northern kingdom of Israel suffered the most and lost most of its territory (2 Kings 15:29).

2. In 722-721 B.C. Shalmaneser V of Assyria besieged the northern kingdom's capital of Samaria (2 Kings 17:5, 6). The city eventually fell to Sargon II, and large numbers of its inhabitants were deported.

3. During the reign of Hezekiah in 701 B.C., Judah unwisely joined a revolt against Assyria. King Sennacherib overran much of the country, but Jerusalem was spared in the end.

Micah's book must be read in the light of these events. The prophet was obviously a keen observer of current events, and God's message to him speaks to his contemporary situation.

Theme and Message

Micah's basic message is clear. God hates and condemns sin—whether it be religious, economic, or social. Because of that sin, God must judge and punish His people. Doom is about to fall. On the other hand, there is hope, because God is merciful, compassionate, and forgiving.

Most people probably know Micah for his three most famous passages:

1. Micah 4:3 (paralleled in Isaiah 2:4), which talks about the peace that will occur when "we shall beat our swords into plowshares."

2. Micah 5:2, which talks about the birth in little Bethlehem Ephrathah of a ruler over Israel. Matthew, of course, quotes this verse in reference to Jesus, the Messiah.

3. Micah 6:8 which says, "He has showed you, O man, what is good. And what does the Lord require of you? To act justly and to love mercy and to walk humbly with your God." This passage has been turned into a popular religious song.

These verses are a good way to remember Micah and his message—peace, (4:3), Messiah (5:2), and justice (6:8). (See Limburg, 159.)

I have chosen to call the book of Micah "Gloom Yet Greater Glory." This theme recognizes the fact of judgment but emphasizes that the restoration God promises through His forgiveness and through the Messiah give Israel a greater glory than she has ever had before. Such is the grace of Micah's God. Who is like Him?

Outline of Micah
Gloom Yet Greater Glory

   I. Heading and Introduction (1:1)
  II. Cycle 1—Judgment and Deliverance (1:2–2:13)
     A. Samaria and Judah lost (1:2-16)
     B. Rich landowners and false prophets condemned (2:1-11)
     C. Deliverance to a remnant (2:12, 13)
 III. Cycle 2—False Leaders and a Righteous Ruler (3:1–5:15
     A. False leaders rebuked (3:1-12)
     B. A righteous kingdom and ruler (4:1–5:15)
 IV. Cycle 3—Israel's guilt and God's forgiveness (6:1–7:20)
     A. Israel's sin and misery (6:1–7:7)
     B. Israel rises by God's forgiveness (7:8-20)

CHAPTER SIXTEEN

False Leaders Fail

Micah 1–4

After a short, one-verse introduction, Micah launches into the heart of his message. From His heavenly holy temple, Yahweh addresses the whole world. All peoples (1:2) are summoned by God to hear a divine indictment against them. From this broad base, the nations of Israel and Judah are specifically singled out, for their sin has come under judgment.

Several groups receive their own special mention: the proud rich who oppress others (2:1-4), the false prophets who are able to prophesy only good things (vss. 6-11; 3:5-7), unjust leaders (vss. 1-4, 9-12), and even priests (vs. 11) are singled out. For Micah, much of the fault of Judah's and Israel's sin lies at the door of these prominent groups. They, of all people, should know better.

In spite of all this, God has not cast His people away forever. Like a shepherd, He will bring His remnant flock together. Included in God's restoration are all peoples who stream toward Mount Zion to find out what God is doing for His people. Let's look now at this story in detail.

■ Getting Into the Word

Micah 1–4

1. **Even though Micah comes from Judah and mentions three rulers of the southern kingdom, his introduction mentions Samaria (capital and representative of the northern kingdom), along with Jerusalem (capital and representative of**

the southern kingdom). Both kingdoms are part of his concern. What parts of these first four chapters refer specifically to the northern kingdom of Israel or Samaria? What parts refer to the southern kingdom or Jerusalem? Are there some parts that refer to both? How do you know?

2. Note the specific sins condemned in 2:1-5. List these sins, and tell what kind of people you think would do these things. How was land regarded (see, for example, Lev. 25:10-13 and Num. 27:1-11)? Why was it so important? What will happen eventually to these people who misuse land rights (see Mic. 2:5)?

3. False prophets are condemned in Micah 2:6-11 and 3:5-7. List the specific wrongdoings of these false prophets. What will be the result of their sins? How do these false prophets compare with the true prophet, Micah (vs. 8)? What does this teach us about the nature of prophecy? On the basis of these passages, how numerous and important do you think false prophets were in Israel during Micah's time?

4. This section of Micah has two "hope" sections: 2:12, 13 and 4:1-13. Compare and contrast these two sections. How are they the same? How are they different? Make a list of similarities and differences. Who is each addressed to? Taken together, what kind of picture of the future do they portray?

■ Exploring the Word

Israel and Judah Under Siege

The Old Testament prophets are surprisingly universal and international in scope. Many of them, including Isaiah, Jeremiah, Ezekiel, and Amos include prophecies that speak to foreign nations. Even the books that do not include such prophecies, such as the book of Micah, very often place their message in an international setting. Although Micah says his vision or prophecy concerns the northern kingdom of Israel (under the symbol of its capital, Samaria) and the southern kingdom of Judah (under the symbol of its capital, Jerusalem) (1:1), he still makes his book international. The message of the book opens with the clear call in verse 2 for all peoples (nations, ethnic/cultural groups) to hear what Yahweh has to say. The Lord witnesses against all as He speaks from His holy temple. Even more, as we will see later, the restoration God predicts in Micah includes more than just Israel and Judah. Micah thus makes it clear that God has the whole world in His thoughts and vision for the future.

After his sweeping international introduction, Micah goes on to speak specifically to God's two-part chosen people. Often it is not easy to tell exactly whom these messages in Micah are addressed to. At times they are clearly to one of the kingdoms, while in some places they seem to apply to both. Some effort at sorting this out does help us understand Micah's message in a clearer way.

After his universal introduction (vs. 2), Micah describes a theophany or appearance of God (vss. 3, 4). The announcement of God's coming is followed by an awesome description of the physical effects of His arrival—melting mountains and splitting valleys. The shock comes in verse 5. Most often in the Old Testament God appears to bring deliverance to His people (see, for example, Judg. 5; Isa. 63; Hab. 3). But in this case, God comes because of transgressions. His coming is not to save, but to call to account those who have sinned.

The ones who have sinned are called "Jacob" and the "house of Israel" (1:5). Samaria seems to be the center of this sin. Here "Jacob" and "Israel" clearly mean the northern kingdom. This is confirmed by the fact that immediately following is the prediction that Samaria, the proud capital of the northern kingdom, will become a heap of rubble with the foundations of her buildings laid bare (vs. 6). Her idolatry caused this, and these false gods will be destroyed in the disaster (vs. 7).

One difficulty is that for Micah "Jacob" and "Israel" do not always mean the northern kingdom. "Israel" is also used for the southern kingdom in 3:1, 8, 9 and 5:1, 3. In 1:14, 15; 2:12; 5:2; and 6:2, the term seems to apply to the whole covenant people of God—north and south. The definition of the word must be determined by the context in which it is used.

As we pick up the thread of the message, Micah bemoans the results of Samaria's sin and fall. Samaria's wound is incurable, and it is affecting Judah (1:9). The picture is of one event leading to another. What has happened to Samaria and the northern kingdom has not left the southern kingdom of Judah unaffected. The problem has come to Jerusalem itself. The impact of this kind of thinking is powerful. Micah will weep and wail, howl, or moan. He will go barefoot and naked to show his deep emotion and feelings of pain (vs. 8).

Although Assyria is not mentioned by name, Micah must know that the agent of God's judgment on Samaria is that powerful nation. The prophecy against Samaria is fulfilled when Samaria falls into Assyrian hands in 722 B.C. The same armies are going to affect Judah as well, and they do in the late 700s B.C. when Sennacherib's troops rumble through Judah.

Micah obviously cares deeply about this impending tragedy. What comes to his mind are the towns, mostly small, of his own home region. He does not want this calamity told to Judah's enemies in the pagan Philistine city of Gath (vs. 10), but he does desire these towns near his own home to know what will happen. In 1:10-15 Micah mentions ten towns (excluding Jerusalem) that will be affected. We don't know where all these towns were located, but the known towns form a circle with a radius of fourteen kilometers around Micah's hometown of Moresheth Gath (Alexander et al., 153). Micah is concerned because this judgment is coming to his own home to roost!

The whole passage features word plays, much like puns, in which the sound of the town's name mimics the sound of the words that predict the doom. Such things are impossible to translate but would be much like saying in English "London will be undone." Many Bibles have marginal references that explain this fact, and those who are interested can discover the details there.

The most prominent of these ten cities was Lachish (vs. 13). It was one of the largest cities in Judah. Sennacherib was so proud of conquering Lachish that he decorated his palace in his capital of Nineveh with a relief showing his accomplishment. Lachish was a key defensive point for Judah. When it fell, Jerusalem was vulnerable, and tribute to Assyria became a necessity.

Micah ends this section by reiterating the need for grief. Not only will these cities be taken and Jerusalem threatened, but many will go into exile as well (vs. 16). The grief Micah calls for is a grief that he himself has already shown (notice the repetition of "I" in verse 8). One cannot help but sense that Micah himself is deeply moved by the impending sense of doom. He has started with the world and has ended up in a very real sense "at home." God's judgment is on the world and on him and his family and territory. What an incentive to preach! What a clear identification of self with the audience! Micah serves as an example to modern, would-be "prophets" and preachers.

Sins of the Leaders

After his initial general condemnation of sin and call to mourning, Micah becomes more specific. In chapters 2 and 3, he takes on the elite and the leaders of God's people, spelling out specific sins.

The first issue is one of land and property (Mic.2:1-5). Although I am not a farmer, both my parents were raised on farms, and thus both sets of grandparents were farmers. I retain a deep love for the land and enjoy gardening and raising fruit. Because of financial problems during the American Depression of the 1930s, my maternal grandfather lost ownership of his land. I can still sense how terrible this made him feel. I thus empathize deeply with those who are victims of ones who "covet fields and seize them, and" who "defraud . . . a fellowman of his inheritance" (vs. 2).

Micah does not specifically name the perpetrators who are stealing land. If we understand the situation at that time, we must say that anyone with the power to openly defraud could be part of the problem. These people are rich and powerful and either part of, or allied with, the nobility and ruling class. They perform these deeds "because it is in their power to do it" (vs. 1b).

What is happening? This rich elite plans and plots evil even in the night at home in bed. The sin is taking the land and houses of people in a dishonest way. Micah 2:4b says this sinful elite defraud their fellowmen of their "inheritance." This "inheritance" refers to the land that each family was to use and possess permanently. Thus both the words *fields* (2:2a) and *inheritance* (2:2b) refer to land—agricultural land in particular.

To fully understand the enormity of what they are doing, we need to understand land and its tenure in Israelite thinking and law. Land really belonged to God. As Owner, He had given it as a gift to Israel. That land was the very source of life. It was not a commodity, but a free blessing from Yahweh to use to get food for existence.

Land was *never* to be sold. How can you sell God's gift? In actuality, specific plots of land were held by tribes and clans and perhaps extended families. Members of tribes, clans, and families by virtue of that membership had rights to use that land. Although Leviticus 25:14 talks of Israelites selling their land, a careful reading of this passage makes it clear that land was not really sold, but rather leased. It could be leased only until the next year of Jubilee, when it reverted to its original "tenants" and was again divided temporarily among individual family or clan members by lot. The land must not be "sold permanently" (Lev. 25:23).

Yahweh says in this passage that because of this illegal seizure, He will give the land to "traitors" (2:4b), probably Assyrians. When they take over the land, no one will be left to divide the land again to Israelites by lot.

As is apparent, this sin is much more than just cheating someone out of their money. It destroys part of God's direct law in connection with land. The whole social and agricultural system is threatened. People are dislocated. A land of free, small-land-holding peasants disappears into a system of absentee, rich, estate owners. Sweeping economic and social change take place.

This sin was probably widespread, since it is also mentioned by Micah's contemporary, Isaiah (5:8). In some places, this evil is connected with the rise of a monarchy. Samuel warned Israel that kingship would bring such situations (1 Sam. 8:14), although, ideally, a renewed, revived monarchy after the exile was forbidden to engage in this practice. The monarchy did bring social change and undoubtedly contributed to land loss, even if it were not totally to blame for it.

Besides the rich land-grabbing elite, Micah takes on the false prophets in two major sections—2:6-11 and 3:5-7. The fact that the first of these sections immediately follows Micah's condemnation of the rich land-grabbers may imply that the two are connected. False prophets may have actually been supporting, or at least silent in the face of, the sinful land deals.

Micah's statements confirm what we hear from other prophets such as Amos (see 7:10-13). Two kinds of prophets and/or priests existed. Those who truly proclaimed and/or ministered for God and another class who were in it for the money and security. These "bought" court prophets and priests were continually at odds with God's true prophets. Not only does Micah battle them, but so do other prophets such as Jeremiah (23:9-40) and Ezekiel (13).

The basic burden of these false prophets seems to be their displeasure with Micah over his preaching of judgment. Micah's clear message that Israel will fall is heresy to them. They do not believe that God is angry and will do such things to His people. They appear to believe that the blessings of the covenant still apply and that Israel's ways are not sinful enough to bring on the promised covenant curses.

The specific words of these prophets are quoted in 2:6, 7a. God's initial response, in question form in verse 7b, is meant to point them back to a full, balanced view of the covenant. True, God has words of blessing, but are those not based on the condition that people obediently respond to God? The clearly implied answer is Yes. If Israel has sinned, the words of blessing turn to curses and judgment.

What exactly have these false prophets done? They do not see, or choose not to see, sin. This blindness to the sin of the people bears results. Israelites are emboldened in their evil. They act like enemies to their fellow Israelites and forcibly take their robes (vs. 8). We are not exactly sure what this means, but most believe it refers to bailiffs who forcibly remove the cloaks of debtors as surety for loans (Allen, *The Books of Joel, Obadiah, Jonah, and Micah*, 297). This fits with the earlier economic context and directly violates Exodus 22:26, 27, which states that if a cloak is taken in pledge, it is to be returned before sunset. That enables its owner to sleep warmly at night, his cloak serving as his only blanket.

Micah's next accusation is even worse. The false prophets' silence has emboldened people to mistreat women (probably widows) and children (orphans?) (vs. 9). These women have been driven from their homes, and their children have lost their rightful heritage. Such actions are specifically forbidden in Exodus 22:22. "Do not take advantage of a widow or an orphan." The Exodus passage goes on to specifically outline the penalty for such action—death. Micah wants his hearers to see that his words are directly based on the revelation of God to His people in the Torah law. They cannot escape judgment, for God has long ago decreed it.

The second passage (3:5-7) directly accuses the false prophets of leading people astray. It thus builds on the accusation of 2:8, 9. These prophets have enabled all this sin because they have falsely proclaimed "peace." Not only that, they have done all this for money. At heart they are mercenary, as both passages make clear. They prophesy to get wine and beer (vs. 11) and speak only if people feed them (3:5; see also verse 11).

The result is that God will desert them. They will lose their vocation and calling. Visions and divination, their means of revelation, will cease (vss. 6, 7). God will no longer answer them. They will lose face and be disgraced. Their people will be judged, and so will they.

In contrast to these false prophets, the true prophet, Micah, will be filled with power and with the Spirit (vs. 8). God will speak to Micah, and he will declare justice—something the other prophets have been missing. He will boldly declare to Israel her sins and transgressions. Studying this passage in Micah, as well as the related passages in Jeremiah and Ezekiel mentioned earlier, convinces me that false prophets were a major problem during the prophetic period. The idea that only true prophets existed and that their main battle was with unrepentant people is false. The picture we get from Micah's book is that there were numerous voices raised in opposition to him and they also claimed to speak for God. For many people it was not clearly obvious who spoke with true divine inspiration. Micah in his struggle to convey truth faced opposition from many angles. Being a prophet has never been easy!

Micah should raise again in our minds the issue of what a true prophet's basic message ought to be. Prophecies of peace, so-called "good" prophecies in Micah's time, were the false ones. Judgment must not be neglected. True prophecy is judged by the covenant that is about both love and justice—about both blessings and cursings. A balanced prophetic message, which clearly and honestly discerns both the sin and righteousness of the time, is called for. Any prophecy that sounds too good—especially if it is proclaimed by "bought" prophets—is dangerous.

Hope for the Remnant

As mentioned earlier, Micah is unique in the way he organized his book. The three cycles of judgment followed by hope sets his work apart. The two passages of hope that we have in our study for this chapter are the first hope section (2:12, 13) and the first section of the second hope cycle (4:1-13). Each section of hope builds on, and then goes beyond, the one preceding it.

The first hope section (2:12, 13) does not specify any time element for the coming deliverance. In Micah's mind the indefinite future probably points to a fairly near future. At this time, God pledges to bring together the remnant of His people. Yahweh behaves as a shepherd who gathers His scattered sheep together. The people are pictured breaking through a gate and going out, with their Lord and King leading the way. While this passage may refer to Israel's later escape from Babylonian captivity, more likely the reference here is to Jerusalem's escape from Sennacherib's siege in 701 B.C. (See Allen, *The Books of Joel, Obadiah, Jonah, and Micah*, 242, 243, 301; Alexander, et al., 160, 161).

The fact that Israel passes through "the gate" (vs. 13) calls to mind the references in 1:9 and 1:12, which speak of the gate of Jerusalem. The Jerusalem that seems to be on the brink of destruction in chapter 1 is delivered from siege in chapter 2. King and people are safe under the Lord, who is their Head.

The second deliverance passage is not only much longer, but also paints a much broader picture of hope (4:1–5:15). This passage actually deals only with about half of this long section. The next chapter will cover the second half of the package. The second deliverance takes place "in the last days" (4:1) and points to a more distant future than the first deliverance passage.

This deliverance section begins with the wonderful moving vision of the mountain of the Lord in verses 1-5. This passage clearly has a close relationship with Isaiah 2:1-4. Scholars have debated as to whether Micah borrowed from Isaiah or vice versa or whether they were both dependent on some third source. No consensus exists on the answer to that question, nor is the answer vital to understanding Micah's message. About all it tells us is that the ideas expressed seem to have been widely known in Micah's day.

What we can say is that Micah did not just find a proof text in Isaiah and drop it in here. There are at least five ways this passage is directly tied to preceding parts of Micah's message.

1. There exists concern for Zion (3:10, 12, and 4:2).

2. In 3:12, the temple hill is plowed and diminished, while in 4:1 the temple hill is a mountain that towers over surrounding hills.

3. The wicked leaders (literally "heads") of the house of Jacob (3:9, 11) are contrasted with the top or chief (literally head) of the mountain (4:1).

4. Micah 3:10 speaks of building Zion with bloodshed and wickedness, while 4:1, 2 speaks of establishing it as a place where people come to learn God's ways.

5. Israel's leaders, priests, and prophets are condemned in 3:11 for teaching and working for monetary gain, while 4:2, 3 shows God as a true Teacher, Judge, and Governor of the nations (Alexander, et al., 166).

The clear message is that what was lost in judgment in chapter 3 will be more than restored or righted in God's renewal portrayed in 4:1-5. Judgment and salvation go closely together.

What does this passage teach us? Note the specific highlights of this future hope:

1. The exaltation of Yahweh's templed presence. The temple on Mount Zion was the center of God's presence. This mountain becomes "chief among the mountains" and is raised "above the hills" (vs. 1). Height was important in the ancient near east. Many places of worship were built on high ground, and mountains were often sacred. This concept is still widespread today; I experienced it widely in my missionary service in Asia. The symbolism is dramatic and clear—Israel's God will be "higher," or more exalted, than any other god, and all peoples will recognize that.

2. *The universal appeal of Israel's religion.* Although Micah began with the command for all peoples (nations) to hear God (1:2), most of what he has said so far applies specifically to Israel. In this passage, he clearly returns to his universal scope. Micah 4:1 speaks of the nations flowing to Zion. The next verse (vs. 2) specifically quotes the nations while verse 3 talks of Yahweh judging the "peoples" and "nations" and settling their disputes. Micah 4:5 again mentions the nations. Clearly, the renewal that God brings affects not only Israel, but the world.

3. *The missionary movement is both centripetal and centrifugal.* Those who view the prophets as "missionaries" to the nations often see this missionary movement as only centripetal, that is, in terms of the nations coming to Israel. The nations are attracted to, and flow to, Jerusalem, or Israel. That centripetal movement is clear in 4:2, which speaks of nations going to Jerusalem. What is also clear from the passage is that something flows *out* as well. The movement is also centrifugal, or going out. The "law will go out" as will "the word of the Lord" (vs. 2b). In that going out, God will judge between the nations and settle disputes. The Missionary God reaches out to bring peace to all. The work of God and His people portrayed here include *both* these vital aspects of mission.

4. *The mission of Yahweh involves both the Word of God and the peace of God.* Yahweh is concerned that people know His Word and law (instruction), which entail cognitive truth and theology, but He is also concerned that they understand, as well, His justice and social concern. God's "ways" or "paths" (vs. 2) contain both evangelism and social concern. The unnatural division between these two aspects does not exist for Micah. God's truth for the nations brings both a knowledge of Yahweh and a new way of living together in peace. Modern-day believers in Jesus would do well to adopt this same teaching!

5. *Those delivered are the downtrodden underdogs.* When God does these wonderful things, who in Israel is the beneficiary? According to Micah, it is the lame, the exiles, and those whom God has brought

to grief and driven away (vss. 6, 7). These unfortunates become God's remnant (vs. 7a) and are turned by God into a "strong nation." God turns the tables. The formerly strong are gone, and the previously weak become a mighty nation. This reversal of fortunes can only be the work of the sovereign Lord. This is Micah's vision of the meek inheriting the earth. The fourth chapter goes on to reassure a concerned Israel that one day a now weak and judged people of God will become strong and will indeed break the foreign nations in pieces (vs. 13).

When does all this take place? From our study of Joel earlier in this book, you will recognize the phrases "in the last days" (vs. 1) and "in that day" (vs. 6) as day-of-the-Lord phrases. You may also recall that Peter, in the book of Acts (2:17), sees Joel's prophecy as fulfilled in the coming of the Spirit. Exactly the same phrase introduces Micah's passage as introduces the Acts passage. This leads us to believe that Peter sees this passage in Micah (and Isaiah) as referring to the new age initiated by Jesus through the church. I cannot help but think that the missionary theology of the New Testament has at least some of its root right here. If prophecies about the coming of the Spirit in the last days were viewed as fulfilled in Acts, so should prophecies of a great turning of the nations to God be seen to be fulfilled in the mighty missionary outreach of the church. As we still believe in the continued need for, and presence of, the Spirit, so we should still believe in the need for the ongoing task of bringing instruction and justice to the nations. We are not finished yet! Micah has more to say about hope in chapter 5. To that we will turn in our next chapter.

■ Applying the Word

Micah 1–4

1. **How does Micah's swinging back and forth between judgment and hope affect you? What effect do you think this had on his readers? Have you heard preachers or teachers present**

sin and salvation in the same sermon or class? Is this good? Does it bring mood swings and confusion, or does it help balance things? Should we combine such topics when we teach God's Word? Why, or why not?

2. How do you feel about the people who live near you? Have you warned them? Do they need warning? What kind of warning? Micah seemed to care a great deal about the towns surrounding him. What can we learn for our own lives from that concern?

3. Micah condemns wealthy land-grabbers who cheat (probably legally) poorer people. Who are such people today? Does land have the same meaning in our society today as it had for ancient Israel? Sharp business deals and deceptive fine print on contracts cheat people. Have you ever been a victim of such things? How did you feel? Have you ever been involved in something similar?

4. Micah, the true prophet, proclaims judgment, while false prophets cry out about peace and make a living off their work. What does this teach us? Are the only true pastors those who proclaim judgment? Are preachers who talk about peace false "prophets"? Are paid religious workers false "prophets"? What should true believers today be preaching? Judgment? Peace? Both? Why? What does the historical situation have to do with the message?

5. Faulty leaders are specifically condemned by Micah. Should we do the same? What faults of leaders should be spoken against? Why? When? What can Micah teach us about the governance of our country and our church? How important is leadership, and how should we work to ensure good leadership?

6. What can Micah 4:1-6 teach us about mission? Is it God's plan today to have non-Christians "flow" to a certain place like Jerusalem? If it is, what place would that be? Should people come to us for teaching, or should we go out to teach them? Should we do both? Does God want to use us to settle disputes for other nations? If so, how should we do that? Is it really part of our mission?

■ Researching the Word

1. Micah shows great interest in the people and geography of his native area. Using a Bible atlas and Bible dictionary or encyclopedia, plot the location of the places mentioned in Micah 1:10-16. If possible, find out exactly where these places are. List the facts you are able to uncover about their history and inhabitants. Do you get the sense Micah has visited these towns? Why?
2. King Hezekiah is important as a background to Micah and to other prophets as well. Read about his life in 2 Kings 18-20, 2 Chronicles 29-32, and Isaiah 36-39. Do you agree with Bible evaluations of his reign? Why? From your reading, what do you think are the most prominent strong and weak points of his reign and character? How does all this help you understand Micah better?
3. Compare Isaiah 2:2-5 with Micah 4:1-5. Note carefully the context of each passage. List similarities and differences between the two. Who do you think wrote this passage first? Isaiah? Micah? Someone else? Give your reasons. What does the existence of these parallel passages teach us?

■ Further Study of the Word

1. As general background to Micah and his message, read what Ellen G. White says in *Prophets and Kings*, 322-339.
2. To get a thought-provoking slant as to how some of Micah's passages might be applied to our modern situation, see Corbett, *Prophets on Main Street*, 121-143.
3. For an in-depth look at Israelite village land tenure and why abuses so upset Micah, see J. Dybdahl, *Israelite Village Land Tenure*. The initial chapter, which explains land tenure and the pages dealing with Micah and Isaiah, are especially helpful.

CHAPTER SEVENTEEN

A Righteous Ruler Reigns

Micah 5–7

The introduction to the book of Micah suggested that it be seen as containing three cycles of doom, each followed by hope for the future. In the last chapter, we stopped in the middle of the "hope" phase of the second cycle. In this chapter, which covers Micah 5–7, we finish the second "hope" cycle and study the concluding "doom-hope" section.

While Micah 4 describes God's plans for the heathen nations and Israel, chapter 5 specifically deals with a coming ruler and the features of his reign. We might aptly call it "King and Kingdom." The nature of the predicted righteous ruler and what it came to mean to Israel and the Christian church are important issues that we will consider.

Before all this takes place, however, God has a court case against Israel. Her "crimes" have to be dealt with and her guilt established before either the hope of chapter 5 or 7:8-20 can become a reality. Before restoration can take place, sin must be faced and dealt with. In the midst of the gloom of judgment, we must remember that God has a future planned that is far better than anything we have ever known.

■ Getting Into the Word

Micah 5–7

1. **Micah 5:1-6 speaks about two rulers. What happens to the first of these rulers in 5:1? Based on what we have said about Micah's history, when might this take place? In contrast, list**

the characteristics of the second ruler as found in 5:2-6. Matthew 2:6 quotes part of this passage. Which part? Why do you think Matthew left some of it out? What does Matthew's use of this passage teach us?

2. The concept of remnant is important to Micah. All three hope sections specifically deal with the topic—see 2:12; 5: 7, 8; 7:18. Read these verses carefully. Write down all the specific facts they teach about the remnant. Why does this concept seem to be important to Micah? What message is in it for us?

3. In Micah 6:1-8, God makes a court case against Israel. Who are the witnesses? What question does God ask Israel? How is it answered? Verses 6 and 7 tell us what will *not* please the Lord or lift the court accusation. List these things. Verse 8 makes clear what God *does* want if the charges are to be dropped. What are these things? Are they difficult to do?

4. One of Micah's accusations is that Judah has "observed the statutes of Omri and all the practices of Ahab's house" (6:16). What does this mean? Use a concordance to find out who Omri was. What were his statutes? Who was Ahab, and why is he mentioned with Omri? Compare your findings with a Bible dictionary. Specifically, what was Israel doing that God disliked so much?

5. Besides the sins mentioned in 6:16, Micah 6:9–7:7 contains a specific summation of other sins committed by Israel. Make a list of these sins. What does this passage tell you about what is important to God? What types of sins seem to be emphasized? Why?

6. The concept of the shepherd is a crucial one to Micah—see 2:12; 5:4, 5; 7:14. Using a Bible dictionary or encyclopedia, find out what the ancient near eastern concept of a shepherd was. Does this idea prevail in Micah, or does he seem to give the idea new meaning? Why does he use this imagery of sheep, shepherd, and flock so often? What is he trying to teach us by its usage?

∎ Exploring the Word

Present and Future Rulers

Micah 5 opens with a brief look at a depressing situation in Israel. She and her ruler are in trouble. This gloom, fortunately, lasts for only one verse, because the next five verses look to a wonderful future ruler and the results of his reign. Let us examine the passage in detail.

If you check a number of Bible versions, you will notice they translate the first part of 5:1 differently. Some translations, such as the KJV and NIV, speak of "marshaling troops," while others talk about being "walled in with a wall" (RSV, NRSV, NEB). Some commentators even suggest the text should read something like, "slash yourself, city of slashers" (see Limburg, 185; Allen, *The Books of Joel, Obadiah, Jonah, and Micah*, 339).

The reason for the differences is that the original Hebrew wording is unclear. However, in the context of the meaning of the passage, any of the above translations make sense. This is because the second part of the verse is clear—Jerusalem is under siege by an enemy. Thus Israel needs to gather its troops (probably the best translation). It is also true, however, that Israel is walled in by the siege and that she may be slashing herself as a typical traditional sign of mourning over her terrible condition.

Not only is Israel's capital under siege, but her ruler is in trouble. The enemy strikes her king on the cheek with a rod. In other words, the king is humiliated. He is so weak and unprotected that he cannot defend even his own face (Job 16:10; Lam.3:30). The rod could also be a scepterlike symbol of authority, and a person who is struck by the rod is clearly subject to the one who strikes. The Israelite ruler, who was to rule the nations with a rod, is now himself struck (see Ps. 2:9) as a sign of his weakness.

Micah clearly identifies himself with this situation by his use of the pronoun "us" in 5:1. What is this referring to? Probably the siege of Jerusalem by Sennacherib and his armies in 701 B.C. The Assyrians are knocking on the door; the future is bleak; the ruler is about to be humiliated.

The scene changes abruptly, and verse 2 begins with that short, but vital, word, *but*. In the midst of doom, hope shines forth. God is going to act on behalf of His people, and there will be a new ruler. Since this passage is so important, we want to look at it in detail. Note the following important points that describe this coming king.

1. This ruler comes from Bethlehem Ephrathah (vs. 2). Ephrathah is mentioned for several reasons. First, to differentiate this Bethlehem from another Bethlehem located in the territory of Zebulon (Josh. 19:15). This passage deals with the Bethlehem in Judah. Ephrathah, ("fruitful"), refers to the Bethlehem area where the Ephrathite clan (where the name probably originated) lived (Ruth 1:2). This is part and parcel of a detailed description that ties the coming ruler closely to David. The book of Ruth deals with the early origins of David's family (see Ruth 4:18-22), and this specific Bethlehem sets the new ruler geographically in the right place for being a true descendant of David's royal line.

2. The clan and the place of origin are "small" (vs. 2). Small, in this case, refers to weak, despised, or even lowly. This Bethlehem is not named in Joshua's list of place names or in Micah's roll of fortified Jewish cities (1:10-15). The place was insignificant, which fits well with the usual way God operates. He likes to choose and use the "small" and insignificant. He chose Gideon, who was the youngest in his family, which was from the weakest of Manassahite clans (Judg. 6:15). David himself was so insignificant in his own family that he was not even called when Samuel came to anoint a king from Jesse's family (1 Sam. 16).

3. The ruler's origins are from "ancient times" (NIV), or "days of eternity" (NIV margin) (5:2). This latter part of verse 2 has been argued over extensively in modern times. Modern versions were attacked when they changed the phrase, "from eternity" (KJV), to translations that seemed to place this Davidic ruler or Messiah within history and recorded time. Some Christians saw this as an attempt to rob Jesus, the Messiah, of His preexistence.

In Hebrew, this phrase is wonderfully ambiguous. It can actually be taken either as "ancient times" or "days of eternity," as is demonstrated by the NIV translation and margin given above. I think most Jews read it as a statement that this ruler's bloodline would go back to David and his family. This predicted king was no upstart of recent origins but went back to the founder of the monarchy and fulfilled God's ancient covenant to David (2 Sam. 7:11-16; Ps. 89:35f). The phrase, however, was stated in such a way that eyes that looked to Jesus and were anointed by the Spirit could read the passage with new insight.

4. *This "Messiah" will rule in the strength and majesty of the Lord His God (5:4).* After a one-verse parenthetical statement that tells Israel she will have trouble until this ruler is born (vs. 3), Micah picks up his description again. The reign of this king will not be in his own power and might. He will be in such a close relationship with God that God's power will be manifested through him. Other rulers may have trusted in military or political power, but this Davidic king truly will rely on God.

5. *The people of Israel will live securely and at peace (vss. 4b, 5a).* Under such a king, the people of God need not worry. They will be secure, and the new king will be their peace.

6. *Enemies of Israel will be vanquished (vss. 5b, 6).* In Micah's time, Israel's main concern was her foreign enemies—especially Assyria. This enemy (also called "the land of Nimrod") will be defeated, and Israel will rule over her through the numerous leaders ("seven shepherds, even eight leaders") that God provides. This is one of the reasons the peace and security mentioned above will become a reality.

7. *This ruler has a universal greatness (vs. 4b).* The Messiah's rule is not confined to the borders of Israel. It goes even beyond Assyria. His reach, according to Micah, is "to the ends of the earth." All nations and peoples are to be affected by the ruler who comes out of Bethlehem.

This passage is vital to the New Testament and to Christians. The most famous and direct quotation of it in the New Testament is found in Matthew 2:6, which we will examine in detail. (We should not forget that it is also used in Ephesians 2:14. Paul seems to have Micah 5:5a in mind when he speaks of Jesus as our peace.)

Matthew 2:6 is a rather loose reference to Micah 5:1-6. It actually uses only verse 2. One could argue also that Matthew's reference to Jesus as a shepherd could be taken from Micah 5:4. Most commentators, on the other hand, see the second half of Matthew's quotation as a reference to 2 Samuel 5:2, where David is clearly referred to as a shepherd.

The emphasis in Matthew is on two main points: (1) Bethlehem as the birthplace, and (2) Jesus' status as ruler. Matthew does not mention Ephrathah; he refers to Bethlehem as being in the land of Judah. Thus Matthew's quotation alters slightly the second clause of Micah 5:2 and uses a portion of 2 Samuel 5:2 as the last clause in the verse.

Matthew seems to be quoting from memory. He uses Micah as a reference to point out that popular Jewish belief of his time looked to Bethlehem as the Messiah's place of origin. The verse in Matthew comes from the lips of the chief priests and teachers of the law (Matt. 2:4). It seems reasonable to believe that as scholars, they would have seen the whole Micah passage (5:1-6) as referring to the Messiah. Christians followed their lead, or Matthew would not have quoted all this approvingly. Although only a small portion of the passage is quoted, the Jews of the first century were familiar with the entire Old Testament section referred to. They would have had in mind the whole passage.

As we look over the seven points about the Messiah that are pointed out in this passage, it is easy to see how all of them could, *in principle*, refer to Jesus. If one merely interprets "Israel" as referring in general to the people of God and "Assyria" as referring to her enemies or Satan, the whole scheme fits. No wonder Jews were so anxious to have this new "Son" of David come. No wonder the early Christians found evidence for their belief in Jesus in these Old Testament prophets and prophecies. Jesus was the answer to all their ancient hopes and needs. He was firmly anchored to the best in the past, but He also went above and beyond what they expected. He was an even better "Messiah" than they hoped.

Of Court Cases and Sins

We leave now the heights of hope personified by the coming messianic Ruler and begin to descend into the valley where the reality of Israel's present situation is made clear. The next "doom" section (6:1–7:7) begins with God's court case against Israel and then enumerates specific sins. We now examine the passages in detail.

This new section of the book begins with an appeal for Israel to listen to what the Lord says (6:1), then Micah begins the lawsuit. Notice the repetition of legal terms in the two brief verses (vss. 1a, 2)—*plead, case* (twice), *accusation,* and *charge.*

Many Old Testament prophets use lawsuit-type language and symbolism in their books. Isaiah (1:2, 3; 18-20; 3:13-15), Jeremiah (2:4-13; 29:31), and Hosea (2:4-13; 4:1-6; 12:3-15) are examples of this. In Micah's case, the plaintiff is God, with Micah as His representative, or lawyer. Israel is the accused, and the witnesses (or perhaps jury) are the ever-present hills and mountains. These "everlasting foundations of the earth" (6:2) are important. They were present as witnesses to God's original covenant at Sinai. They know what God has done for Israel (vss. 4, 5). Their enduring nature and continual witness remind Israel of where she has come from and where she is now. They are fair witnesses and an honest jury.

God's charge against Israel comes in the form of two questions: "My people, what have I done to you? How have I burdened you?" (vs. 3). The implication is that Israel has abandoned her God and broken her covenant (a legal agreement) with Him. What has God done to deserve or provoke this? Is He in some way responsible for this breach of contract? God says, "Answer me!" (vs. 3). This is not the voice of an enemy but of a loving husband who still calls Israel "My people."

God then proceeds to spell out all the good things He has done for His people (vss. 4, 5). Chief among these is the Exodus, followed closely by the provision of good leaders like Moses, and then providential protection. Israel must remember these things and recognize God's grace.

In the face of this charge and the recitation of God's goodness in her history, Israel must respond. She does in verses 6 and 7. Her answer takes the form of questions, just as God's accusation of her has done.

In the light of God's court case, what can Israel do to fix things? What Israel (and perhaps especially the king, because only royalty could bestow gifts of the magnitude mentioned here) suggests is a cultic response. Israel wants to fix things by the ritual of sacrifice. These sacrifices increase in magnitude with each of the four progressive steps suggested in the questions. Will God be satisfied with (1) burnt offerings of year-old calves? (2) thousands of rams? (3) ten thousand rivers of oil? (4) one's own first-born child?

The implied answer comes thundering back, "NO! A thousand times no!" Israel shows the depth of her sin by the terrible misunderstanding manifested in her questions. She wants to buy her way out of the court case! She wants to assuage her guilt by ever-bigger and more costly sacrifices. She has forgotten that the covenant is a relationship and that all God's good gifts in her history were acts of sovereign grace done in love without cost. There is no way she can "sacrifice" herself out of her sin and guilt.

Micah himself must respond. Israel has the wrong answer, so God through Micah (vs. 8) provides the true answer to what is good and what God requires of His people. The answer is brief and threefold: (1) "Act justly," (2) "love mercy," (3) "walk humbly with your God." Look a bit more closely at these three elements of goodness.

"Act justly," or literally in Hebrew, "to do justice," is the first requirement. The word translated "justly," or "justice" (*mishpat*), means first of all to practice the requirements of the law that relate to other people. Beyond this, it requires a relationship that gives back what is due and even goes on to deliver the oppressed and downtrodden. The requirement is relational, ethical, and concerned for others' welfare. The prophet does not directly condemn all cultic sacrifice but clearly points to an ethical concern and justice toward others as more basic to God's covenant.

Second, God calls for people who "love mercy," or, literally, "love covenant faithfulness." The Hebrew word *hesed*, which is behind the NIV translation "mercy," is a most important word for explaining the nature of the covenant and its spiritual obligations (Waltke, 734). The term assumes a covenant relationship and connotes the fact of deliverance or protection of another as a way of being faithful to their mutual covenant. The English Bible uses many different terms to translate this one Hebrew word, which is so full of meaning. These include: favor, goodness, kindness, loving-kindness, merciful kindness, mercy, and kindly. The concept of mercy or kindness is involved because covenants were often between parties that were not equal. In general society, a superior person was *not* obligated to help or have mercy on an inferior one. But in covenant relationships that was expected. That kindness was *hesed*, or covenant kindness. This kind of attitude was what God wanted Israel to have in her midst. He not only wanted her to have it, but as Micah says, to *love* it. He had shown that kind of attitude toward Israel, and He expected her to have the same feeling toward other people, following His example.

God's third and final requirement was to "walk humbly" with God. In this third requirement, we are not dealing with the horizontal human-to-human relationships referred to in the first two obligations. This requirement deals with the vertical, human-to-divine part of the covenant relationship.

In the KJV and NIV, the word *humbly* could be better rendered as *wisely* or *circumspectly* (Waltke, 735). Israel had been very unwise in her relationship to God. Part of that was due to a lack of wisdom and understanding of the very nature of the covenant. This has just been manifested in verses 6 and 7 of this chapter, where Israel wants to assuage her guilt by sacrifices. What Israel needs is to truly understand who God is, what He has done and will do for Israel, and the nature of His covenant relationship with her. This is walking wisely with God.

What happens next in the passage is that Micah points out specific instances as to how Israel has *not* been following these three basic requirements. Proper covenant relationships with other humans and with God have been violated. In essence, this is Micah's way of producing evidence that God's lawsuit is a valid one. We now want to look at 6:9–7:7 to find out exactly what these sins are so we can clearly see the truth of God's charges and the depths of Israel's waywardness.

The specific sins of Israel seem to be clustered around several main points.

1. Sins of dishonesty. This sin is manifested in at least two ways. The first is cheating in business, which includes shortchanging people ("short ephah," vs. 10) and the use of dishonest scales and weights (vs. 11). This is the source of some ill-gotten treasures (vs. 10a). The second way is lying with tongues that speak deceitfully (vs. 12).

2. Sins of the leaders. The rich and powerful are "violent" (vs. 12a), which refers to their oppressive treatment of the poor that has been spoken of earlier (2:1, 2). Whatever the powerful want, they get (7:3b). The rulers and judges demand gifts and accept bribes (vs. 3a). In this way, the poor have no place they can go for justice.

3. Sins of violence. Not only are the rich and powerful violent, as mentioned above, but the common people have joined in. "*All men* lie in wait to shed blood and *each* hunts his brother with a net" (vs. 2, emphasis supplied). Certainly crime waves are not a modern invention!

4. Sins among friends and family. In the midst of all this, relationships with those who should be close and trustworthy have broken down. You can no longer trust your friends and neighbors (vs. 5). The Hebrew word translated "friend" in verse 7 means "intimate friend." You can't even have confidence in those closest to you. The same is true of family. Even the spouse who lies in your embrace must be spoken to in a guarded way (vs. 5b). The sons and daughters of your own household have become enemies (vs. 6). In a time when everything seems to be going wrong, you would hope that family could be a refuge. Micah's words make it clear that is not so.

5. Sins against God. The first four major categories of sin we have just described are against human beings. They represent disruptions in human-to-human relationships. Micah also refers to religious sins.

Judah is observing the "statutes of Omri," and following "Ahab's house" (6:16). These things, Micah says, have led to Israel's ruin and her derision by the surrounding nations. What exactly are these sins?

Omri was a ruler of the northern kingdom of Israel about one hundred years before Micah. He founded a dynasty and eventually passed on the kingdom to his more famous son, Ahab. These two kings are the only ones named in the prophetic books, aside from the introductory statements to the various books (McComiskey, 742).

These two kings were famous for their wickedness, but we must remember this passage is not talking about these two kings alone. Micah 6:16 says, "Ahab's house," which includes his family and dynasty. Ahab's wife, Jezebel, is well-known for her evil ways and Baal worship. She threatened to kill the prophet Elijah (1 Kings 19:2). Coming from a Canaanite background as the daughter of the king of Tyre, she vigorously promoted her idolatrous beliefs in Israel. The wicked queen Athaliah, who attempted to slay the Davidic royal line, was a daughter of Ahab (see 2 Kings 8:18; 11).

How galling it must have been for Judahites to be told they were like a dynasty known for wickedness, one which had even tried to kill their own royal house! This must have been part of Micah's shock treatment for Judah and an attempt to wake her up.

Probably this comparison of Judah to Ahab is made for another reason besides the general state of religious apostasy it is portraying. Ahab and Jezebel are also famous for the Naboth incident (1 Kings 21). By plotting, deceit, and finally murder of an innocent man, they procure land that they desire. This act seems to parallel what has been seen in Micah, where rulers and leaders steal money and land by dishonesty and violence.

These five major areas of sin not only show us Israel's fallen state, but also demonstrate direct opposition to what God has said He requires in Micah 6:8. Justice, mercy, and wise walking with God are exactly what Judah has *not* been doing in following the five kinds of evil practices outlined here. The charge against Israel is valid, therefore the sentence is justified. Judgment can come because there is ample reason for it to be expected.

A Final Restoration

Fortunately for Judah, the judgments meted out on the basis of God's "trial" of Judah are not God's final word, or Micah's either. Micah 7:8-20 portrays a restoration for Israel. She has fallen, but she will rise (vs. 8). She has been in darkness, but the Lord will bring her out into His light (vs. 9). God will have compassion on her and deliver her from destruction, captivity, and her enemies. God will keep His covenant, which He made with Abraham and Jacob (vs. 20), and Israel will become all that God plans for her to be.

The nations of the world will be affected. Some of these nations will come to Israel (vs. 12), while others will simply look on in amazement, and because of what they see, will turn in fear to God (vss. 16, 17). Israel's restoration will have a worldwide impact. Since God is fulfilling His oath to Abraham, which included a blessing on all the nations, all this is only the natural fulfillment of God's pledges of long ago (vs. 20).

Embedded in this final restoration passage are two themes or ideas that occur not only here, but in numerous places in the book. A closer look will help us understand more fully the restoration God promises through Micah.

The first of these themes is the remnant. All three restoration sections in Micah make mention of this idea (see 1:12; 5:7, 8; 7:18). What does the remnant mean for Micah, and why does he use the concept? An overall view of the book makes it easier to understand this.

As has been explained already, because of Judah's sin, Micah expects her to fall very soon. Destruction and ruin are imminent. The natural question is how all this relates to the idea that Israel, as God's chosen people, will be a great nation. Will Israel remain as a nation? The clear answer is that many in Israel will be destroyed but that God will save some and start over. The remnant idea then speaks to the issue at hand. In the light of Israel's sin and judgment, will she go on? The answer is Yes. A remnant, a small portion, will be spared to be restored and to receive God's covenant promises. Thus the remnant is the key to the continuity of God's people.

In the first hope passage, note some of the specific characteristics of the remnant. The remnant are those whom God gathers together (2:12). The implication is that they have been scattered like sheep and had to be brought together as a flock and given safety. The clear emphasis is that the Lord will do this and no one else—note the threefold "I will" of verse 12. The divine Shepherd will bring back and care for His remnant flock.

The next hope passage (5:7, 8) is in some ways similar, but the text adds some ideas. The remnant is scattered among many people. This was implied in the earlier passage, but is clearly stated here—three times in fact (vss. 7a, 8). What the passage emphasizes is that with divine help, Israel will be like a lion that destroys its prey (vs. 8b). Of course, God is really the one who does this—note verses 10-19 and the fourfold repetition of "I will destroy," referring to God's action. The reason for this is the sin and lack of obedience of these nations (vs. 15b).

In the final restoration section, the remnant are those who receive the pardon and forgiveness of God for their sin (7:18, 19). God's anger at their sin is over. Because of His compassion, He throws all their sins into the depths of the sea. The covenant-keeping God shows mercy, just as He pledged to do long ago (vs. 20). God keeps His promises!

Interestingly enough, Micah prefaces this passage on God's merciful, compassionate, forgiving actions with a play on words. It stems from the meaning of the prophet's own name, Micah. You remember that his name means "Who is like God." Note the first phrase of Micah 7:18 (NIV), "Who is a God like you?" This kind of mercy is such that no one else but God can possess it. For Micah, that is the essence of what God is like—and a great way for him to bring his book to a conclusion!

In summary, we have a moving picture of the remnant scattered among the nations by sin and the resulting judgment. But the Lord is going to gather this remnant together. He will bring her into one flock. In compassion, He will forgive her sins and pardon her iniquity. In the process, the sin of the world will be made manifest, and God will judge the nations for their disobedience. Through the remnant, God will be true to the covenant promises He has made long before to Abraham and Jacob.

A Royal Shepherd

One other major theme, which also occurs in all three hope sections of Micah, will reward us as we study it. This is the subject of shepherds and their role. We will note, in turn, Micah 2:12; 5:4, 5; and 7:14, and conclude with some general observations on shepherds and shepherding in the ancient near east.

In Micah 2:12, the delivering Yahweh is pictured as a shepherd. Israel is like a "flock in its pasture," and they are brought "together like sheep in a pen." Yahweh will "go up before them," leading the way by being at their head (vs. 13).

In the second deliverance passage, the messianic ruler from Bethlehem is compared to a shepherd with his flock (5:4). Later he has helpers in "seven shepherds, even eight leaders of men" (vs. 5) who help deliver God's people. The grammatical rules of Hebrew poetry with its parallelism imply that "shepherds" and "leaders" are synonymous. Shepherds *are* leaders.

In the final "hope" passage in 7:14, the shepherd again is Yahweh. With His staff (scepter?), He leads Israel, His flock, to pleasant pastures. He does wonders for them as He did during the Exodus (7:15). Nations are amazed at what He does.

Two false pictures of Old Testament shepherds exist in the minds of most western peoples. Our culture tends, first of all, to picture shepherds as primarily pastoral, in the caring, nurturing sense. While this is not false, and is certainly a part of what being a shepherd meant in the ancient near east, another image dominated. First of all, shepherds were rulers. Kings and leaders are shepherds. God is thus the foremost Shepherd, and His ruling representatives are shepherds also. In ancient times, kings demonstrated their legitimacy to rule by their ability to properly pasture their "sheep," or people. Both in the Psalms and in Micah, God as shepherd takes care to pasture His flock. The shepherd's staff functions as a royal scepter—a sign of ruling power.

In western culture, shepherds follow their flock and *drive* them. In the Old Testament, shepherds *go before* their flock and *lead* them (note especially Mic. 2:13 and Ps. 23:2). The shepherd stands in front of the flock calling it to follow him to green pastures, not behind it pushing and prodding.

This background enriches our understanding of Christ the Good Shepherd portrayed by John in chapter 10 of his gospel. John is trying to do much more than simply portray the loving care of Jesus. As the Good Shepherd, Jesus is a messianic ruler like Yahweh. He has power and authority to care for His sheep. The "flock" is secure because this powerful leader will make sure that none of His flock are lost. He stands at the front of His flock calling to them and urging them to follow.

That is really the same picture Micah leaves with us. Israel may be a battered flock standing under judgment, but God will restore her. The scattered remnant will be gathered by the all-powerful Shepherd. She will be compassionately forgiven and become God's flock, carefully pastured forever in the most fertile of meadows. What a hope for Israel! Who is like this God?

■ Applying the Word

Micah 5–7

1. Israel needed a new leader/ruler. Does your nation need new leadership? Does your church? In Micah's day there were real problems with corruption and sin in leaders. Do we see the same today? Where? How important is leadership to a nation or church? How should Christians react to poor leadership?
2. What passages from this part of Micah speak to you most powerfully? The coming Messiah? God's requirements in Micah 6:8? God's forgiveness in 7:18-20? Some other passage? Why is this passage important to you? How does it apply to your life?
3. Does God have any court cases against you? Against your church? If God were to bring a court case against you or your church, what do you think the charge would be? Whom

would God call as witnesses? What evidence would He use? What would be your defense? Would it be inadequate like Israel's, or adequate? Why?

4. What would be the "practices of Ahab's house" (6:16) today? Where have we, without thinking, become like enemies of the faith? How would people respond today if preachers accused them of following after famous sinners? What does this passage warn us to be careful of in our life today?

5. In Micah, God is not pleased with simply offering many "sacrifices" to get rid of sin. Do people today do anything similar? Can even good religious practices become rituals designed to "buy" forgiveness? What Christian practices could easily become like "thousands of rams," or "rivers of oil" (6:7)? How can we guard against this problem?

6. What can Micah's presentation of the remnant contribute to how we view the remnant? According to Micah, how is remnant status achieved? What is the duty of the remnant? What does "remnant" imply about out past, present, and future?

7. Micah has a powerful portrayal of God's forgiveness in 7:18-20. God not only shows mercy, but, according to Micah, "delights" (7:18) to show it. If you really believed God *delighted* in showing mercy to you, how would you feel? Would you hold anything back in your relationship? Wouldn't you go to Him with your sins and your needs? What does it mean to you to have God "tread our sins underfoot" and "hurl our iniquities into the depth of the sea" (6:19)? Have you experienced that? If not, just take a minute, and picture Him doing that as you confess what stands between you and Him.

■ Researching the Word

1. As has been pointed out, *remnant* is an important word to Micah. It is, however, not unique to him. Other prophets also used the term. Using a concordance such as Young's *Analytical Concordance*, find how other prophets, especially Isaiah, used the word. Read the passages where the word is

used, and see if you can find any new ideas connected with the word that Micah does not contain.

2. Another important word to Micah is *shepherd*. Again, using a concordance, find all the passages that refer to shepherds. Note especially those that seem to use the term in a symbolic sense as referring to God or others who are not literally shepherds. What do you find that adds to your knowledge of how Old and New Testaments utilize this word?

3. A third word that teaches us much about God and our relationship to Him and to others is the word *hesed* or *chesed*. Micah 6:8 translates this word as "mercy," but as this chapter suggests, the meaning is much broader. To explore that breadth of meaning, you need to find out the different ways the word is translated into English, and then look up the texts using those words. The easiest way to do that is to find a comprehensive English concordance such as Young's, Strong's, or the *NIV Exhaustive Concordance* that lists Hebrew and Greek words and gives their various translations. For example, in the back of Young's concordance is a Hebrew lexicon section that lists all the differing English translations for the word *chesed*. For Strong's or the *NIV Exhaustive Concordance*, look up "mercy," and then use the numbering system in the back of the book to find the various English words used to translate *chesed* or *hesed*. This may take a bit of time, but you will be richly rewarded, and you will be doing a word study based on the original language.

■ Further Study of the Word

1. You have done a personal Bible study of the remnant. Now read the *SDA Bible Dictionary* on "remnant" and R. Rice, *The Reign of God*, 230, 231, and learn what they have to say.

2. For a more in-depth look at the mercy and forgiveness of God, see Dybdahl, *Old Testament Grace*, especially 83-99.

3. Compare what this book says about the message of Micah with W. S. La Sor, et al., *Old Testament Survey*, 359-364. What are the similarities? Differences?